Wheels and Wilderness

The Ultimate RV Guide to National Park Adventures

Mark Thompson

Table of Contents

INTRODUCTION

Welcome to an unparalleled journey where the unspoiled splendor of America's National Parks is just waiting to be discovered and the open road calls. We cordially invite you to take an incredible journey through the center of our country's most treasured natural wonders with "Wheels and Wilderness: The Ultimate RV Guide to National Park Adventures," all from the comfort of your very own home on wheels.

For those who crave the thrill of adventure as well as the serenity of the great outdoors, there is no better way to experience the majesty of America's National Parks than in an RV. This thorough guide is your ticket to exploring the untamed beauty of our nation's treasures, whether you're an experienced RVer or a newbie looking to get your feet wet.

We'll travel the twisting roads that lead to famous locations like Yosemite, the Grand Canyon, Yellowstone, and more in these pages. We'll find the lesser-known parks and undiscovered treasures that provide peace amid the splendor of nature. We'll provide helpful advice on choosing an RV, organizing trips, staying safe, and being environmentally conscious to make your travels pleasurable and responsible.

Therefore, "Wheels and Wilderness" will be your reliable companion, guiding you through the breathtaking scenery and life-changing experiences that await on your RV adventure, whether you're dreaming of a cross-country road trip, a family adventure, or a solo expedition into the wilderness. Together, let's embrace the freedom of the open road and roll into the wild. This is where the best RV guide to National Park adventures starts.

CHAPTER I

Choosing the Right RV

Types of RVs (Class A, B, C, trailers, etc.)

Recreational vehicles (RVs) have long been a sign of freedom and adventure, offering a unique way to explore the world while enjoying the comforts of home. RVs come in different shapes and sizes, each designed to meet to different needs, preferences, and travel styles. This section will delve into the primary types of RVs, namely Class A, Class B, Class C, and trailers, shedding light on their distinctive features and advantages.

Class A RVs, often referred to as motorhomes, are the behemoths of the RV world. These are the largest and most luxurious options available, resembling a bus in appearance. Class A RVs offer spacious interiors with all the amenities you'd find in a modern home. They boast fully equipped kitchens, full bathrooms, living areas, and comfortable sleeping quarters. Some even come with slide-outs, which expand the living space when parked. Class A RVs are ideal for those seeking a "home on wheels" experience with ample space for large families or groups of friends. They provide a smooth and comfortable ride on the road, but their size can make maneuvering in tight spaces a challenge.

Class B RVs, or camper vans, represent the compact end of the spectrum. These vehicles are essentially converted vans that have been customized to accommodate the necessities of life on the road. Class B RVs are more maneuverable and fuel-efficient than their larger counterparts, making them an excellent choice for solo travelers or couples seeking for an intimate adventure. While they may lack some of the space and amenities of Class A RVs, Class B motorhomes are versatile and can easily navigate urban areas, offering the flexibility to park in standard-sized parking spaces.

Class C RVs bridge the gap between Class A and Class B, offering a combination of space and maneuverability. They have an attached sleeping area that stretches over the cab and are constructed on a truck or van chassis, giving them a unique appearance. Class C RVs typically have amenities like kitchens, bathrooms, and living areas, making them suitable for families and small groups. Their cab-over design provides additional sleeping space or storage and is often more affordable than Class A RVs.

Trailers, on the other hand, offer a diverse range of options. Some of the most common trailer types are travel trailers, fifth wheels, pop-up campers, and toy haulers. Travel trailers are towed behind a vehicle, providing a separate living space that can vary from basic to luxurious. Fifth wheels are similar but are towed by a pickup truck utilizing a specialized hitch that connects to the truck's bed. Pop-up campers are compact and simple to tow, expanding into larger living spaces when parked. Toy haulers combine living quarters with space for recreational vehicles like motorcycles or ATVs, catering to adventure enthusiasts. Trailers offer the advantage of being able to unhitch the living quarters and explore the local area without needing a separate vehicle.

Each type of RV comes with its own set of advantages and trade-offs, allowing travelers to choose the one that best suits their preferences and needs. Class A RVs offer unparalleled luxury and space, while Class B and C RVs provide greater mobility and versatility. Trailers, with their diversity, cater to a wide range of outdoor enthusiasts. Ultimately, the choice of RV type depends on individual preferences, budget, and the kind of adventure one seeks. Whether it's cruising the open road in a Class A motorhome, exploring remote destinations in a Class B camper van, or towing a travel trailer to camp beside a serene lake, the world of RVing offers endless possibilities for exploration and discovery.

Factors to consider when selecting an RV

Choosing the right recreational vehicle (RV) is crucial in embarking on your journey of adventure and exploration. RVs come in various shapes, sizes, and configurations, each catering to different lifestyles and travel preferences. To make an educated decision, several essential factors must be considered when selecting an RV.

The first factor to contemplate is your RV's purpose and intended usage. Are you planning short weekend getaways, extended road trips, or full-time RV living? Your purpose will dictate the size, features, and amenities your RV should have. For instance, a compact camper van may be ideal for weekend trips, while a Class A motorhome or a larger travel trailer might suit those planning extended adventures.

Budget is crucial in the decision-making process. RVs come at various prices, from affordable entry-level models to high-end luxury options. Establishing a budget is critical to narrowing down your choices and avoiding financial strain. Remember that the initial cost is not the only expense; you'll also need to budget for maintenance, insurance, fuel, and campground fees.

Size and layout are also crucial considerations. RVs vary significantly in size and layout, so considering your comfort and spatial requirements is crucial. Consider the number of travelers and whether you need separate sleeping areas, a full kitchen, a bathroom with a shower, and a living or dining space. The layout should match your lifestyle and preferences, ensuring your RV feels like a home away from home.

Another critical decision is whether to go for a towable RV, including a travel trailer or fifth wheel, or a motorized RV, like a Class A, B, or C motorhome. Towable RVs require a separate tow vehicle, while motorized RVs are self-propelled. Your choice will based on your comfort level with towing and the kind of adventure you envision. Towable RVs offer flexibility in terms of the vehicle you use to tow them and can be more cost-effective, while motorized RVs provide a more integrated driving and living experience.

Consider what amenities and features are essential for your RV. RVs offer a wide array of options, ranging from basic to luxurious. Do you want a fully-equipped kitchen, a large bathroom, entertainment systems, slide-outs for added space, or solar panels for off-grid living? Prioritize your needs and desires to find the RV that best suits your lifestyle and travel aspirations.

For those concerned about fuel efficiency, especially for extended journeys, it's essential to consider the RV's mileage. Class B and C motorhomes tend to be more fuel-efficient than larger Class A motorhomes. Smaller travel trailers are also more economical in fuel consumption, saving you money in the long run.

Maneuverability is another practical consideration. Think about where you plan to travel and park your RV. Larger Class A motorhomes can be challenging to navigate in urban areas and fit into smaller campsites, whereas Class B and C motorhomes, along with smaller travel trailers, offer greater maneuverability in tight spaces. Ease of parking and accessibility to your desired destinations should play a role in your decision.

Storage and cargo capacity are essential for stowing away camping gear, outdoor equipment, and personal belongings. Some RVs provide ample storage solutions, while others may require you to pack more selectively. Ensure that the RV you choose has enough cargo space for your necessities to avoid clutter and inconvenience during your travels.

Maintenance and repairs are practical considerations as well. Consider your capacity and willingness to perform maintenance and repairs on the RV. More complex motorhomes may require professional servicing, while more straightforward travel trailers might be easier for the owner to maintain. Factor in the cost as well as availability of maintenance services when selecting your RV.

Lastly, think about the resale value of the RVs you're considering. RVs depreciate over time, but some models hold their value better than others. Research the resale value of the RVs in your shortlist to make an informed investment decision, considering the long-term financial aspects of RV ownership.

In conclusion, selecting the right RV is a pivotal decision that can significantly impact your travel experience. By carefully considering factors like purpose, budget, size, layout, amenities, fuel efficiency, maneuverability, storage, maintenance, and resale value, you can narrow down your options and find an RV that perfectly aligns with your travel aspirations and lifestyle. Remember that your RV should not only be a means of transportation but also a comfortable and enjoyable home on wheels, enabling you to explore the world with ease and enthusiasm.

Budgeting and financing options

Starting an RV adventure is an exciting journey, but it needs careful financial planning to ensure that your dreams of open-road exploration align with your budget.

Understanding budgeting and financing options is essential for a successful and stress-free RV lifestyle, from purchasing your RV to covering ongoing expenses.

Setting a realistic budget is the initial step in your financial journey toward RV ownership. Your budget should encompass not only the cost of the RV itself but also the associated expenses, such as insurance, maintenance, fuel, campsite fees, and other incidentals. When setting your budget, consider your financial situation, income, savings, and long-term goals. Determining your budget will assist you narrow down your options as well as guide your decisions throughout the RV buying and ownership process.

Financing an RV is a common approach for those who may not have the full purchase price readily available. Many lenders, including banks, credit unions, and RV dealerships, offer RV loans with various terms and interest rates. To secure the best financing option, it's essential to keep a good credit score and provide proof of income and financial stability to possible lenders. Additionally, exploring different lenders and comparing loan offers can help you find the most favorable terms and rates for your situation.

One financing option to consider is an RV-specific loan, tailored to RV buyers' unique requirements. These loans often have longer terms, allowing for lower monthly payments, and may offer more flexibility regarding down payments and interest rates. However, it's necessary to carefully read and understand the terms and conditions of any loan agreement to avoid unexpected costs and fees.

Another financing route to explore is refinancing an existing asset, such as your home, to secure a lower-interest loan for your RV purchase. Home equity loans and/or lines of credit can provide a source of funds for buying an RV with more favorable terms compared to traditional RV loans. However, this approach may involve placing your home as collateral, which carries its own risks.

Leasing is an alternative to traditional RV ownership and financing. With an RV lease, you essentially rent the RV for a specified period, typically several years. While leasing may result in lesser monthly payments compared to loan payments, it's essential to understand the limitations and restrictions that come with a lease agreement. These can include mileage limits, wear and tear guidelines, and restrictions on customization. Leasing may be suitable for those who want to enjoy an RV without committing to long-term ownership.
Aside from financing the RV purchase, budgeting for ongoing expenses is crucial for maintaining your RV lifestyle. Monthly expenses include RV insurance, fuel, campground fees, maintenance, and repairs. RV insurance is a legal requirement, and its cost can vary depending on elements such as the RV's value, usage, and your driving history. Comparing insurance quotes from various providers can help you find the most affordable and comprehensive coverage for your RV.

Fuel costs are a significant portion of an RV owner's budget and can vary greatly depending on the RV's size and fuel efficiency. Smaller, more fuel-efficient RVs generally offer savings at the pump, while larger motorhomes may have higher fuel consumption. Careful route planning, driving at moderate speeds, and utilizing fuel-saving technologies can help reduce fuel expenses.

Campground fees can also vary widely, with options ranging from free boondocking sites to upscale RV resorts with amenities like swimming pools and entertainment. Planning your travel itinerary and researching campgrounds in advance can help you budget for accommodation costs effectively. Many RVers also use membership programs and discount clubs to access reduced campground fees.

Maintenance and repairs are inevitable expenses when owning an RV. Regular maintenance, such as engine checks, tire rotations, and appliance inspections, is essential to keep your RV in good condition and prevent costly breakdowns. Creating a maintenance schedule and budgeting for routine service can help you avoid unexpected repair bills down the road.

In conclusion, budgeting and financing are integral aspects of RV ownership and the RV lifestyle. Establishing a realistic budget, exploring financing options, and planning for ongoing expenses are essential to ensure that your RV adventure is enjoyable and financially sustainable. By understanding your financial situation, exploring financing alternatives, and carefully managing ongoing costs, you can embark on your RV journey with confidence and peace of mind, knowing that your financial foundation is secure.

CHAPTER II

Planning Your National Park Adventure

Researching National Parks

Embarking on an RV adventure to explore America's National Parks is a dream for many outdoor enthusiasts. The vast and diverse landscapes, breathtaking natural wonders, and rich biodiversity found within these protected areas offer a lifetime of exploration and discovery. However, planning an RV trip to National Parks requires thorough research to ensure a rewarding and well-prepared experience.

The first step in your journey to National Parks in an RV is conducting comprehensive research about the parks themselves. The United States boasts an extensive system of National Parks, each with its unique characteristics, attractions, and regulations. To make the most of your adventure, you must prioritize which parks to visit and understand their specific features.

Identify the National Parks that align with your interests and travel route. Whether you're drawn to the geothermal wonders of Yellowstone, the towering cliffs of Zion, or the pristine wilderness of Denali, each park offers a distinct experience. Consider factors such as the time of year you plan to visit, the activities you enjoy, and your desired level of solitude. Some parks are best explored during the peak summer season, while others shine in the quieter months of spring or fall.

Once you've chosen your target National Parks, delve into the park-specific details. The National Park Service (NPS) website is a valuable resource, providing a multitude of information on each park's history, geography, wildlife, and attractions. Be sure to explore the NPS website's individual park pages to find visitor center locations, trail maps, camping information, and alerts about road closures or park conditions.

Understanding the park's regulations and fees is essential for a smooth RV adventure. National Parks may have specific rules regarding camping, hiking, and recreational activities, so it's crucial to familiarize yourself with these guidelines. Additionally, parks may require entrance fees or camping reservations, which can vary depending on the park's popularity and amenities. Booking your campground reservations well in advance is advisable, especially for popular National Parks during peak seasons.

Incorporating the National Parks Passport program into your research can enhance your RV adventure. At each National Park you visit, you can obtain official park stamps and cancellation marks with the National Parks Passport, a convenient booklet that can be purchased at park visitor centers. Collecting these stamps is a delightful way to document your travels and a keepsake to cherish for years to come.

While researching National Parks, it's also essential to plan for the specific needs of your RV trip. RV campgrounds within National Parks vary in terms of amenities, so consider whether you require full hookups, electrical hookups, or can comfortably dry camp without hookups. Be prepared with the necessary RV supplies, including leveling blocks, hoses, and extension cords, to ensure a comfortable stay.

Before setting out on your RV adventure, check the National Park's accessibility and RV length restrictions. Some park roads may have height, width, or length limitations that could impact your travel plans, so ensure your RV is suitable for the routes you intend to take. Additionally, inquire about any seasonal road closures, as some park roads may be inaccessible during winter.

Safety is a top priority when exploring National Parks in an RV. Research the weather conditions and potential hazards in each park, especially if you plan to visit during the offseason. Additionally, familiarize yourself with wildlife safety guidelines to minimize encounters with wild animals. Properly store food and trash to prevent attracting wildlife to your campsite, and always respect park regulations regarding wildlife viewing and interactions.

Finally, connect with the National Park community to gain insights and tips from fellow RVers who have experienced these magnificent destinations. Online forums, RV travel blogs, and social media groups dedicated to National Park enthusiasts can provide valuable information and recommendations for an unforgettable RV adventure.

In conclusion, researching National Parks is crucial in planning your RV adventure. By thoroughly understanding the parks you intend to visit, their regulations, and the specific needs of your RV trip, you can ensure a rewarding and well-prepared experience. National Parks offer abundant natural beauty and outdoor activities, and with the right research and preparation, your RV adventure will be a memorable journey into the heart of America's wild and protected landscapes.

Creating an itinerary

Creating an itinerary that maps out your journey across diverse landscapes and destinations is one of the most exhilarating aspects of planning an RV adventure. Whether you're a seasoned RVer or embarking on your first RV expedition, crafting a well-thought-out itinerary is essential for maximizing your experience, staying organized, and ensuring that you don't miss out on the incredible sights and experiences along the way.

The first step in creating an itinerary for your RV adventure is to establish your trip's overall theme or purpose. Are you seeking a leisurely exploration of National Parks, an adventure-packed road trip along the coast, or a journey to reconnect with nature in remote wilderness areas? Your trip's purpose will guide your route and help you prioritize the destinations and activities that align with your goals.

Once you have a clear purpose, consider the duration of your RV adventure. Determine the days or weeks you have available for travel and allocate time for driving, sightseeing, and relaxation. Remember that long driving stretches can be tiring, so balance your itinerary with enough downtime to recharge and enjoy the journey. Researching your desired destinations is crucial for crafting a well-rounded itinerary. Identify the National Parks, cities, attractions, and points of interest you want to visit along the way. Consider the distance between each location and the estimated travel time, factoring in the pace of RV travel. Remember that RVs typically travel more slowly than passenger cars, and driving can be physically demanding, so avoid cramming too many activities into a single day.

Consider the time of year you plan to embark on your RV adventure. Seasonal variations can significantly impact your travel experience, with some destinations shining in specific seasons. For instance, National Parks exhibit distinct beauty throughout the year, from vibrant spring blooms to the golden hues of autumn. Be mindful of weather conditions, road closures, and any seasonal activities or events that may influence your itinerary.

Flexibility is key when creating an RV itinerary. While planning is essential, leave room for spontaneity and unexpected discoveries along the way. Some of the most memorable moments in RV travel occur when you deviate from your planned route to explore a hidden gem or connect with fellow travelers. Embrace the freedom that RV travel offers, and allow for detours and adjustments to your schedule.

When crafting your itinerary, balance must-see attractions and leisurely exploration. While cramming your schedule with famous landmarks and tourist hotspots is tempting, don't forget to allocate time for quiet moments in nature, leisurely hikes, or simply relaxing by the campfire. RV travel allows you to savor the journey, so don't rush from one destination to the next without taking time to appreciate the beauty of the road itself.

Camping is a fundamental aspect of RV travel, and planning your campground reservations is vital, especially during peak travel seasons. Research campgrounds in advance, considering their locations, amenities, and availability. Some National Parks offer RV-friendly campgrounds with stunning natural settings, while private campgrounds may provide additional comforts like full hookups, laundry facilities, and recreational activities. Make campground reservations well in advance to protect your preferred spots, especially at popular destinations.

To ensure a smooth and safe RV adventure, perform thorough pre-trip inspections and maintenance checks on your RV. Verify that your RV is in excellent working condition, including the engine, tires, brakes, and all essential systems. Carry crucial tools, spare parts, and a first-aid kit to handle common issues that may arise during your journey. Knowing that your RV is road-ready will give you peace of mind and reduce the likelihood of unexpected setbacks.

Communication is essential when creating an RV itinerary. Give your travel dates and destinations to dependable friends or family members by sharing your itinerary with them. Keep your lines of communication open, particularly if you intend to travel to remote areas with poor cell service. Having a dependable way to communicate in an emergency, like a satellite phone or Personal Locator Beacon (PLB), can be extremely helpful.

In conclusion, creating an itinerary for your RV adventure is an exciting and essential part of the journey. By defining your trip's purpose, researching destinations, considering seasonal factors, embracing flexibility, and striking a balance between planned activities and leisurely exploration, you can craft an itinerary that enhances your RV travel experience. Remember that RV travel is about more than just reaching your destinations—it's about the incredible journey you undertake along the way, discovering new places, connecting with nature, and making lasting memories on the road.

Making campground reservations

Making campground reservations is one of the most crucial aspects of planning a successful RV adventure. As an RVer, your home on wheels relies on the availability of suitable campsites to provide you with a comfortable and enjoyable experience. Whether you're a seasoned traveler or new to the world of RVing, understanding the ins and outs of reserving campgrounds is essential for a stress- free journey.

The first step in the process is researching campgrounds that align with your travel itinerary and preferences. Campgrounds come in various types and settings, ranging from National Park campgrounds surrounded by pristine nature to privately-owned RV resorts with luxurious amenities. Consider the kind of experience you seek— whether it's a secluded, back-to-nature retreat or a lively campground with social activities—and select campgrounds accordingly.

Once you've identified potential campgrounds, it's essential to check their availability and reservation policies. Many campgrounds, especially those within National Parks and popular destinations, have limited space and high demand, making advance reservations a necessity. Begin your research well ahead of your planned travel dates, as some campgrounds accept reservations up to a year in advance. Early booking is particularly crucial if you intend to travel during peak seasons or even holidays when campgrounds tend to fill up quickly. When making reservations, be prepared to provide specific details about your RV, such as its size and the type of hookups you require (e.g., electrical, water, sewer). Accurate information ensures you're assigned an appropriate campsite to accommodate your RV comfortably. Additionally, inquire about campground amenities, such as Wi-Fi access, laundry facilities, and recreational activities, to ensure they meet your needs and preferences.

Consider the length of your stay at each campground. While some campgrounds offer short-term stays for a night or two, others may have minimum stay requirements, especially during busy seasons. Plan your itinerary accordingly to meet these requirements and allocate enough time to explore the surrounding area and enjoy the campground's amenities fully.

Flexibility is key when making campground reservations. While advanced planning is essential, leaving room for spontaneity and unexpected changes in your travel schedule is also advisable. Circumstances may arise that necessitate altering your reservations, such as unfavorable weather conditions, road closures, or discovering a new, exciting destination along the way. Campground reservation policies may vary, so be sure to inquire about cancellation or modification options and fees when making reservations.

Consider campground fees in your budgeting and financial planning. Campground rates can vary widely depending on location, amenities, and the type of RV site (e.g., standard, premium, or full hookup). Additionally, some campgrounds may offer discounts for seniors, military personnel, or RV clubs and associations members. Explore these opportunities to reduce your camping costs and make your RV adventure more affordable.

Communication with campground staff is essential when making reservations and during your stay. Be clear about your arrival time, especially if you anticipate arriving after the campground's office hours. Some campgrounds have late check-in procedures, while others may require you to arrive during specified hours. Maintaining open and courteous communication with campground staff ensures a smooth check-in process as well as a pleasant stay.

During your RV adventure, it's crucial to practice good campground etiquette. Follow campground rules and regulations, respecting quiet hours, campfire restrictions, and waste disposal guidelines. Treat fellow campers with courtesy and respect their privacy. Be mindful of noise levels, keep your campsite tidy, and properly dispose of trash to contribute to a pleasant camping atmosphere for all.

Lastly, embrace the sense of community that often comes with RV camping. Strike up conversations with fellow campers, share travel stories and tips, and consider joining campground activities or group outings if they align with your interests. RV campgrounds are fantastic places to connect with like-minded travelers and create lasting memories together.

In conclusion, making campground reservations is vital to planning your RV adventure. Thorough research, early booking, accurate information, flexibility, budget considerations, and respectful communication with campground staff and fellow campers are key to a successful camping experience. Remember that the right campground can enhance your RV adventure, providing a comfortable base to explore the natural beauty and attractions while connecting with the vibrant RV community.

CHAPTER III

Essential Gear and Supplies

Packing lists for RV trips

Packing for an RV trip is a unique endeavor that requires careful consideration of the essentials and luxuries you'll need while traveling and camping in your home on wheels. Whether you're a seasoned RVer or embarking on your first RV adventure, creating a well-thought-out packing list is essential for a comfortable, organized, and enjoyable journey.

The initial step in creating a packing list for your RV trip is to consider the specific needs of your travel companions and the destinations you plan to visit. Consider the number of travelers, ages, and special requirements or preferences. Additionally, research the weather conditions and activities at each destination, as this will influence the clothing and gear you need to pack.

Start with the basics, like clothing, toiletries, and personal items. Pack clothing suitable for the expected weather, but also include versatile pieces that can be layered for comfort in various conditions. Don't forget essentials like underwear, socks, sleepwear, and comfortable shoes appropriate for walking as well as outdoor activities. Toiletries should include soap, shampoo, toothbrush, toothpaste, and any prescription medications. Consider the limited storage space in your RV, and bring only what you'll realistically use.

Kitchen and dining supplies are a significant part of your RV packing list. RVs typically come equipped with a kitchen, but you must bring cookware, utensils, dishes, and cleaning supplies. Opt for space-saving cookware and non-breakable dishes to maximize your storage space. Plan your meals and grocery list to ensure you have the ingredients for your preferred recipes.

When it comes to bedding, consider the sleeping arrangements in your RV. RV mattresses may not provide the same level of comfort as those in your home, so bringing your own bedding, including sheets, blankets, and pillows, can enhance your sleep quality. Consider packing sleeping bags or extra blankets for chilly nights or outdoor adventures.

Entertainment and recreational gear can elevate your RV trip experience. Depending on your interests and destinations, bring items like board games, playing cards, books, or outdoor equipment such as hiking gear, bicycles, kayaks, or fishing gear. These items can provide entertainment and enhance your ability to enjoy the great outdoors.

Safety and emergency supplies are essential for your peace of mind during an RV trip. Ensure you have a first-aid kit with basic medical supplies and medications, a flashlight, batteries, and a multi-tool or camping knife. RVs should also be equipped with safety essentials like smoke detectors, fire extinguishers, as well as carbon monoxide detectors.

Utilities like water hoses, sewer hoses, and electrical cords are essential for hooking up your RV at campgrounds. Be sure to include these items on your packing list and any adapters or extension cords you may need for various campground setups. It's advisable to have backup hoses and cords in case of unexpected issues.

One aspect of RV packing that sets it apart from traditional travel is considering outdoor comforts. Outdoor furniture, such as folding chairs and tables, can provide a comfortable place to relax and dine outside your RV. Don't forget items like a portable grill or campfire cooking equipment for outdoor meals and campfires.

In addition to the basics, RV-specific items are essential for a successful trip. These include leveling blocks or ramps to ensure your RV is on an even surface, wheel chocks to prevent rolling, and a water pressure regulator to protect your RV's plumbing system. A surge protector can safeguard your RV's electrical system from power surges at campgrounds.

Organization is key when packing for an RV trip. Utilize storage containers, bins, and shelves to keep your belongings tidy and accessible. Label containers to quickly locate items and efficiently use your RV's available storage compartments and cabinets. Over-the-door organizers and collapsible storage solutions can maximize space in tight quarters.

Finally, embrace the RV lifestyle by packing items that improve your comfort and enjoyment on the road. Bring cozy blankets, throw pillows for a homey atmosphere, and outdoor mats or rugs to create a comfortable outdoor living space. Decorate your RV with personal touches, such as photos or artwork, to make it feel like your own home away from home.

In conclusion, packing for an RV trip is a meticulous yet rewarding task. A well-thought-out packing list ensures you have all the essentials and comforts you need for an enjoyable adventure. By considering the specific needs of your travel companions, the destinations you plan to visit, and the unique requirements of RV travel, you can create a comprehensive packing list that sets the stage for a memorable and comfortable journey in your home on wheels.

Must-have camping gear

When planning an RV trip, having the right camping gear is essential for ensuring a comfortable, safe, and enjoyable journey. Whether you're an experienced RVer or new to the lifestyle, the right equipment can make all the difference. Here's a list of must-have camping gear to consider for your next RV adventure.

First and foremost, outdoor chairs and tables are crucial for creating a comfortable outdoor living space. Folding camping chairs and tables provide you with a place to relax, eat, and socialize outside your RV, making the most of the great outdoors. Look for chairs with features like cup holders and armrests for added convenience.
A camping grill is another must-have item for RV trips. It allows you to prepare meals outdoors, whether you're grilling burgers, cooking breakfast, or roasting marshmallows for s'mores. You can choose between propane or charcoal grills, depending on your preference.

In addition to a grill, having your cookware and utensils is a smart move. While RV kitchens come equipped with the basics, bringing your pots and pans, knives, cutting boards, measuring cups, and utensils can provide you with added flexibility and convenience in the kitchen.

An outdoor mat or rug serves multiple purposes at your campsite. It offers a clean and comfortable area to sit, walk, or relax outdoors, and it helps keep dirt and debris from entering your RV. Choose a mat that's easy to clean and weather-resistant.

Leveling blocks are essential for RV stability and comfort. They allow you to raise or lower the wheels of your RV to achieve a level surface, ensuring that appliances and systems inside your RV function correctly.
Water and sewer hoses are crucial for proper water and sewer connections at campgrounds. Invest in high-quality

hoses to ensure a reliable and leak-free hookup to campground utilities. A dedicated potable water hose is essential for connecting to freshwater sources.

Electrical adapters and extension cords are necessary to accommodate varying campground electrical hookups. These adapters enable you to connect your RV to different types of electrical outlets, while extension cords ensure you can comfortably reach the hookup.

A surge protector is necessary to protect your RV's electrical system from power surges. It monitors the electrical supply at the campground and prevents damage to your RV's appliances and electronics.

Safety is paramount during RV travel, so having an emergency kit is crucial. Include items like a first-aid kit, flashlight with extra batteries, a multi-tool or camping knife, and a fire extinguisher. Having a basic tool kit for minor RV repairs is also a good idea.

Outdoor recreation equipment, such as hiking gear, fishing equipment, bicycles, or kayaks, can enhance your outdoor experiences while on an RV trip. Depending on your interests and destinations, consider packing these items to immerse yourself fully in the outdoor adventures along the way.

Finally, be sure to pack weather-appropriate clothing, including rain gear, warm layers, and lightweight, breathable clothing. These items will assist you stay comfortable and prepared for changing weather conditions during your RV journey.

In conclusion, having the right camping gear is crucial for a successful as well as enjoyable RV trip. Whether you're cooking outdoors, relaxing at your campsite, or staying safe and prepared for emergencies, these must-have items enhance your comfort and convenience while embracing the RV lifestyle. By carefully packing and organizing your gear, you can confidently embark on your RV adventure, knowing you have everything you need for a memorable journey.

Safety equipment

Safety should always be a top priority when embarking on an RV trip. While the RV lifestyle offers freedom, adventure, and the opportunity to explore new destinations, it's essential to be prepared for various situations and emergencies that may arise on the road. To ensure a safe and enjoyable RV journey, having the right safety equipment is crucial. This section will discuss the must-have safety equipment for RV trips, covering everything from fire extinguishers to communication devices.

One of the most critical pieces of safety equipment in any RV is the fire extinguisher. RVs are equipped with kitchens, stoves, and electrical systems, all posing potential fire hazards. A functioning fire extinguisher within easy reach can distinguish between a minor incident and a catastrophic event. Ensure that your fire extinguisher is appropriately rated for RV use, and check it regularly to confirm that it is in good working condition. Smoke and carbon monoxide detectors are necessary for RV safety. Colorless and odorless, carbon monoxide is created by RV appliances such as heaters and stoves. On the other hand, smoke detectors are crucial for detecting fires or smoke inside the RV. These detectors can provide early warnings and are vital for alerting you to potential dangers while you sleep or go about your daily activities. A

well-stocked and up-to-date first-aid kit is a fundamental piece of safety equipment for RV trips. Accidents can happen anywhere, and a comprehensive first-aid kit can guide you deal with minor injuries and provide essential medical care until professional help arrives. Ensure your kit includes bandages, antiseptic wipes, adhesive tape, scissors, tweezers, pain relievers, and any necessary prescription medications.

Emergency communication devices are critical for staying connected and seeking assistance in case of emergencies. While cell phones are a primary means of communication, their reliability can be limited in remote areas or during emergencies. Therefore, having a backup communication device, like a satellite phone or a Personal Locator Beacon (or PLB), is advisable. These devices can transmit distress signals and your location to rescue services, ensuring that help is on the way when you need it most.

Another important safety consideration for RV trips is tire safety. Blowouts and tire failures can lead to accidents, so it's crucial to have the right equipment to address such situations. Ensure that your RV has a spare tire, a tire jack, and the tools for changing a flat tire. Additionally, a tire pressure monitoring system (TPMS) can provide real-time tire pressure and temperature information, alerting you to possible issues before they become emergencies. In the event of a breakdown or mechanical problem, having basic tools and equipment can be invaluable. A basic tool kit that has wrenches, screwdrivers, pliers, and a multi-tool can help you address minor repairs or mechanical issues. It's also wise to have duct tape, zip ties, and spare fuses on hand. These versatile items can temporarily fix various problems until you can reach a repair facility.

A reliable flashlight with extra batteries is essential for navigating dark areas or conducting repairs at night. In addition to a standard flashlight, consider having headlamps or lanterns to provide hands-free illumination. Good lighting can make a significant difference when dealing with emergencies or nighttime situations.

Weather-appropriate clothing and gear are often overlooked aspects of safety. You may experience extreme weather conditions depending on your travel destination and the time of year. Packing warm layers, rain gear, and appropriate clothing for various temperatures can help you stay comfortable and safe while on the road.

Emergency exit tools can be a lifesaver in the event of an accident or emergency that hinders your ability to exit the RV through conventional means. These tools, such as window breakers and seatbelt cutters, can help you and your passengers escape the RV quickly and safely.

RVs should also be equipped with safety equipment such as wheel chocks to prevent rolling, stabilizer jacks for stability, and leveling blocks for proper leveling. These items are essential for maintaining a stable and secure environment within the RV.

In conclusion, safety equipment is a crucial aspect of RV travel that should not be overlooked. From fire extinguishers and detectors to communication devices and emergency tools, having the proper safety equipment onboard can help you address potential hazards and emergencies while on the road. Prioritizing safety ensures you can enjoy your RV adventure with peace of mind, knowing that you are prepared for any situation that may arise during your journey.

CHAPTER IV

RV Maintenance and Safety

Pre-trip inspection checklist

An exciting journey full of exploration and novel experiences awaits those who take an RV trip. However, before hitting the road, ensuring that your RV is in excellent working condition is crucial for a safe and trouble-free journey. A pre-trip inspection is a comprehensive checklist of tasks that should be completed before every RV trip. This inspection not only helps prevent breakdowns and emergencies on the road but also ensures that you have a smooth and enjoyable journey.

The first step in your pre-trip inspection should involve examining the exterior of your RV. Check the condition of the tires, like the tread depth and tire pressure. Examine the condition of the spare tire and look for any indications of damage or uneven wear. Verify that the turn signals, brake lights, taillights, and headlights on your vehicle are all operating properly. Check the mirrors for proper adjustment, and ensure that all awnings, slide-outs, and exterior storage compartments are securely closed and latched.

A thorough inspection of the engine and the chassis is essential for motorized RVs. Verify the levels of the coolant, brake fluid, transmission fluid, and engine oil. Make sure the battery connections are tight and check the battery terminals for corrosion. Make sure the parking and foot brakes are working properly by testing them. Check to make sure there are no leaks visible beneath the

RV and that all of the hoses and belts are in good working order.

Moving inside the RV, conduct a detailed interior inspection. Start with the electrical systems, checking that all interior lights, outlets, and appliances are operational. Test the heating and cooling systems to guarantee they provide adequate temperature control. Examine the plumbing system, including faucets, sinks, toilets, and showers, for any leaks or malfunctions. Test the LP gas system for proper stove, oven, and refrigerator operation. Inspect the carbon monoxide and smoke detectors to ensure they are functioning and have fresh batteries.

Ensure that all safety equipment is in good working order. This includes checking the condition of fire extinguishers and confirming that they are within their expiration dates and fully charged. Check the functionality of carbon monoxide detectors and smoke detectors, replacing batteries if necessary. Ensure that all emergency exit windows and doors can be easily opened, and that emergency exit tools, such as window breakers and seatbelt cutters, are accessible.

If your RV uses propane, carefully inspect the propane system. Ensure that all LP gas lines and connections are free from leaks and in good condition. Test the LP gas appliances for proper operation, including the stove, oven, water heater, and furnace. Turn off the gas supply right away and get expert help if you smell gas leaks or detect a strong propane odor.

Thoroughly inspect the RV's water and waste systems. Look for any obvious leaks or indications of damage in the tanks holding fresh water and wastewater. Confirm that all faucets, showers, and toilets are functioning correctly. Ensure that the sewer hose and connections are in good condition and that there are no blockages or obstructions.

Returning to the exterior, pay close attention to the wheels and brakes. Verify that the lug nuts on all wheels are properly tightened to the manufacturer's specifications. Inspect the condition of the brake pads as well as rotors, looking for any signs of wear or damage. Ensure that the wheel bearings are adequately lubricated and adjusted.

Inspect the suspension and its components, including shocks, springs, and sway bars. Ensure that they are in good condition and properly secured. Verify that the suspension system is adjusted for your RV's load and weight distribution, which can impact stability and handling.

Examine the RV's electrical system, including all wiring and connections. Make any required repairs and keep an eye out for any frayed or loose wires. Test the functionality of all electrical outlets, switches, and appliances. Ensure that circuit breakers and fuses are correctly sized and properly labeled.

Before hitting the road, gather all essential documents and items, such as your driver's license, RV registration, insurance documents, and trip itinerary. Ensure you have a road atlas or GPS navigation system, a tool kit, and essential RV supplies like leveling blocks, wheel chocks, and hoses.

In conclusion, a thorough pre-trip inspection is crucial in ensuring a safe and enjoyable RV journey. By diligently following a pre-trip inspection checklist, you can identify and deal with possible issues before they become emergencies on the road. Regular inspections help maintain your RV's reliability and functionality, allowing you to focus on the adventures and memories that await you during your RV travels.

Safety precautions on the road

Embarking on an RV trip is a thrilling adventure that provides the freedom to explore new places while enjoying the comforts of home. However, it's crucial to prioritize safety on the road to ensure a secure and enjoyable journey. Safety precautions for RV trips encompass various aspects of preparation and driving behavior.

First and foremost, maintaining the RV is paramount. Regular inspections as well as maintenance checks should be conducted before every trip to ensure the vehicle is in excellent working condition. This includes examining the engine, brakes, tires, lights, and all essential systems to prevent potential breakdowns on the road.

Proper loading and weight distribution within the RV are critical for stability and handling. Overloading the vehicle can affect its balance and performance, so it's essential to distribute weight evenly and secure items inside cabinets and storage areas to prevent shifting during travel.

If you're towing a trailer or another vehicle, adhere to towing safety guidelines. Ensure the towed vehicle is properly connected, and all safety chains and hitch components are secure. When towing, be mindful of the longer stopping distance and factor in more stopping time.

When driving an RV, safe driving techniques are essential. An RV needs to be handled carefully because of its size and weight. It's critical to keep a safe following distance from other vehicles and to be conscious of blind spots. Frequent use of mirrors and cautious navigation of sharp curves and narrow roads are also important considerations.

Controlling speed is vital for safety. Driving at an appropriate speed, adhering to posted speed limits, and reducing speed during adverse weather conditions are all essential. On steep descents, downshifting can help maintain control and prevent brake overheating.

RVs require a longer distance to come to a complete stop than smaller vehicles, so understanding your RV's braking system is essential. Braking should be proactive to avoid abrupt stops that can destabilize the RV.
Tire safety is often overlooked but crucial. Maintaining proper tire pressure and inspecting tires for wear, damage, or cracking is necessary for safety and fuel efficiency. Adequate attention should also be given to the spare tire.

Weather conditions can significantly impact safety. Staying informed about weather conditions along the route and adjusting travel plans accordingly is essential. Extra caution is needed when driving in adverse conditions such as rain, snow, ice, or fog.

Managing rest and fatigue is critical for driver safety. Long hours on the road can lead to fatigue, impairing reaction times and decision-making. Regular rest stops and sharing driving duties with a co-driver can help combat driver fatigue.

Emergency preparedness is a must, with an emergency kit that includes items like a first-aid kit, flashlight, batteries, and basic tools. Having a plan for common RV emergencies, such as flat tires or minor mechanical issues, is also advisable.

GPS navigation systems designed for RV travel can provide information on RV-friendly routes, campgrounds, and points of interest. Keeping your GPS updated is essential to reflect current road conditions and construction.

Respecting local laws and regulations is a straightforward yet vital safety measure. Familiarize yourself with state and local traffic laws and RV-specific regulations in the areas you plan to visit. Compliance with these rules ensures a smoother and safer journey.

In conclusion, safety precautions on the road are essential for a successful and enjoyable RV trip. You can explore the highways and byways with confidence and peace of mind by adhering to vehicle maintenance, proper loading, and safe driving practices. These precautions protect you and your passengers and enhance the overall enjoyment of your RV adventure as you explore new destinations as well as make lasting memories on the open road.

Troubleshooting common RV issues

Recreational vehicles, or RVs, have gained immense popularity in recent years as a means of experiencing the freedom of the open road while still enjoying the comforts of home. However, like any complex machine, RVs are not immune to issues and breakdowns. Whether you're a seasoned RV enthusiast or a newcomer to the world of mobile living, it's crucial to understand and be able to troubleshoot common RV problems. In this section, we will explore some of the most prevalent issues RV owners face and discuss practical solutions to keep your adventure rolling smoothly.

One of the most frequent concerns for RV owners is electrical problems. RVs rely on various electrical systems to power lights, appliances, and essential devices. When your lights flicker, outlets stop working, or appliances don't function correctly, it can be a frustrating experience. To troubleshoot electrical issues, check your RV's main power source, typically a shore power connection or a generator. Ensure it's properly connected and functioning. If the problem persists, inspect the circuit breakers and fuses in your RV's electrical panel. Often, a tripped breaker or a blown fuse can be the culprit. Replacing a blown fuse and/or resetting a tripped breaker can resolve many electrical problems.

Another common issue RV owners face is plumbing problems. Leaking pipes, clogged drains, and malfunctioning toilets can turn a relaxing trip into a stressful ordeal. To tackle plumbing issues, first, inspect all visible plumbing connections for leaks. Tighten any loose fittings and replace damaged hoses or pipes. If your RV's toilet is not flushing correctly, it might be due to a waste tank or plumbing system clog. Use a specialized RV toilet treatment to break down waste and prevent clogs. Additionally, take into account using a water pressure regulator to protect your RV's plumbing from high campground water pressures, which can lead to leaks and bursts.

Heating and cooling problems can also disrupt the comfort of your RV. If your heater or air conditioner is not working correctly, start by checking the thermostat settings. Ensure it is set to the desired temperature and mode (heating or cooling). If the problem persists, inspect the air filter in your HVAC system. A dirty or clogged filter can minimize the efficiency of your heating or cooling unit. Regularly replacing or cleaning the filter is essential for maintaining a comfortable interior temperature. If the issue persists, it may be because of a faulty thermostat, a malfunctioning compressor, or low refrigerant levels, which may require professional repair.

Tire-related issues are a significant concern for RV owners. A flat tire or blowout can quickly ruin your trip and pose a safety risk. Make sure your RV's tires are correctly inflated to the recommended pressure, which can be found on a sticker inside the vehicle or in the owner's manual, to avoid tire issues. Look for evidence of wear on the tires, such as cracks, bulges, or irregular tread. Replacing tires that show signs of damage or excessive wear is crucial to avoid blowouts. Additionally, consider investing in a tire pressure monitoring system (TPMS) to receive real-time alerts about tire pressure and temperature abnormalities while on the road.

RVs come equipped with various appliances and systems; issues with these components can also arise. Refrigerator malfunctions, water heater problems, and issues with the RV's slide-out rooms are examples of challenges you may encounter. To troubleshoot such problems, consult your RV's user manuals for specific guidance and troubleshooting steps. Basic maintenance, such as cleaning coils, checking gas supply, or lubricating slide-out mechanisms, can resolve these issues.

In conclusion, troubleshooting common RV issues is essential for a smooth and enjoyable travel experience. Electrical, plumbing, heating and cooling, tire, and appliance-related problems can all be addressed with a combination of preventive maintenance and troubleshooting techniques. Familiarizing yourself with your RV's systems, having the necessary tools and spare parts on hand, and being patient and methodical when diagnosing and fixing problems are key to keeping your RV adventures trouble-free. With the right knowledge and preparedness, you can maximize the enjoyment of your RV lifestyle while minimizing the inconvenience of common issues.

CHAPTER V

National Park Etiquette

Leave No Trace principles

The allure of the great outdoors beckons many to embark on RV adventures, offering the chance to explore natural wonders while enjoying the comforts of home on wheels. However, with the increasing popularity of RV travel comes the responsibility to minimize our environmental impact. Leave No Trace principles, originally developed for backcountry camping, are equally relevant and essential for those embarking on RV journeys. This section will explore these principles and discuss how they can be applied to RV travel to ensure that we preserve and protect the natural world for future generations.

The first Leave No Trace principle is to plan ahead and prepare. For RV adventurers, this means researching your destinations, understanding local regulations, and choosing campsites wisely. Select campgrounds and RV parks that are environmentally responsible and follow sustainable practices. Make reservations in advance to reduce overcrowding at popular sites and contribute to preserving the natural environment.

The second principle is to travel and to camp on durable surfaces. In the context of RV travel, this translates to staying on designated roads and campsite pads. Avoid driving or parking on fragile ecosystems, such as wetlands, meadows, or desert environments, where the impact of heavy vehicles can be particularly damaging. Stick to established trails when exploring on foot, and resist the temptation to create new paths that can erode the landscape.

Minimizing campfire impact is the third principle of Leave No Trace. RV travelers should use established fire rings or designated fire areas, and always follow local regulations regarding open flames. Consider using a camp stove for cooking, as it is more environmentally friendly and reduces the risk of wildfires. Be diligent in properly extinguishing fires and never leave them unattended.

The fourth principle is to dispose of waste properly. RVs come equipped with waste disposal systems, but using them responsibly is essential. Empty gray and black water tanks only at designated dump stations, not on the ground or in natural water sources. Dispose of trash in provided receptacles and, if camping in remote areas, pack out all trash, including food scraps and litter, to avoid attracting wildlife and polluting the environment.

The fifth principle, respecting wildlife, is particularly relevant to RV travelers. It's necessary to observe wildlife from a safe distance, even though it can be tempting to get up close. Feeding wild animals can harm both humans and the animals themselves, as it disturbs their natural behavior. Food should be kept out of the reach of wildlife to lower the chance of habituation and conflict.

Leave No Trace's sixth principle emphasizes minimizing campsite impact. For RV travelers, this means leveling your RV on established pads and avoiding the use of leveling blocks that can damage the ground. Use minimal impact camping techniques, such as setting up a camp kitchen on a tarp to catch spills and prevent soil compaction. Leave your campsite as you found it, or even better, by removing any signs of your presence.

The seventh and the final principle is to be considerate of other visitors. RV travel often involves close proximity to other campers, so it's essential to maintain a respectful and quiet atmosphere. Keep noise levels down, especially during quiet hours, and respect the privacy and space of fellow travelers. Yield the right of way on narrow roads and trails, and be mindful of the impact of your activities on others' enjoyment of the outdoors.

In conclusion, RV travel can provide a unique opportunity to interact with nature while enjoying the comforts of home. However, with this privilege comes a responsibility to comply with Leave No Trace principles to preserve the environment and leave our natural world unspoiled for future generations. By planning ahead, treading lightly, and respecting nature and fellow travelers, RV adventurers can minimize their impact and ensure that the beauty of the outdoors remains for all to enjoy. Embracing Leave No Trace principles enhances the RV experience, fostering a more profound connection with the natural world and promoting responsible stewardship of our planet's treasures.

Rules and regulations within National Parks

National parks are natural treasures that offer unparalleled opportunities for RV adventurers to connect with the great outdoors. However, specific rules and regulations must be followed to preserve the beauty and integrity of these protected landscapes. These guidelines ensure the safety of visitors, protect fragile ecosystems, and maintain the pristine condition of these national treasures. In this section, we will explore the crucial rules and regulations that RV enthusiasts should be aware of when embarking on an adventure within national parks.

One of the most fundamental rules within national parks is adhering to park hours and entrance fees. Most national parks have set operating hours to manage visitor flow and protect wildlife during critical periods. It's essential to check the park's official website or visitor center for up-to-date information on operating hours and entrance fees.

Paying the required entrance fee not only helps fund park maintenance and conservation efforts but also provides visitors with valuable access to park resources and amenities.

Once inside the national park, RV travelers should be aware of the specific regulations governing camping and RV use. Many parks offer designated campgrounds where RVs can park, while others may restrict camping to certain areas. Making reservations well in advance is crucial, as campgrounds in popular national parks often fill up quickly. Additionally, campers should be aware of generator use regulations, quiet hours, and waste disposal. Dump stations are typically available within the park for emptying RV waste tanks, and adherence to these guidelines is essential to maintain the cleanliness and beauty of the park.

When exploring national parks with an RV, following established road and parking regulations is crucial. Stay on designated roads and pullouts to prevent damage to fragile ecosystems and ensure other visitors' safety. Oversized RVs may have restrictions on certain park roads due to size limitations or tight turns, so it's essential to research and plan your route accordingly. In some cases, shuttle buses or guided tours may be the best way to explore specific areas within the park, especially if you are traveling with a large RV.

National parks also have specific rules regarding outdoor activities, such as hiking and wildlife viewing. Visitors should remain on marked trails and avoid off-trail hiking to protect delicate vegetation and wildlife habitats. Keep a safe distance from wildlife, as close encounters can be dangerous for humans as well as animals. Giving food to wildlife is forbidden, as it can disrupt natural behaviors and harm animals. Rangers and park staff provide valuable information and guidance to help visitors make the most of their outdoor experiences while preserving the park's integrity.

Given the potential for wildfires in natural areas, fire regulations are paramount in national parks. Open fires may be restricted during certain times of the year or in specific areas due to fire danger. RV travelers should know fire restrictions and use camp stoves or designated fire rings when allowed. Always fully extinguish fires before leaving a campsite and follow park guidelines for fire safety.

In some national parks, pets are welcome, but strict rules govern their presence to protect wildlife and other visitors. Keep pets on a leash at all times, clean up after them, and adhere to designated pet-friendly areas. Some parks may have restrictions on certain trails or areas where pets are not allowed.

Finally, leave no trace is a universal principle that applies in all national parks. This means packing out all trash, following the "pack it in, pack it out" philosophy. Dispose of waste in designated receptacles and recycle whenever possible. Respect natural and cultural features by not picking plants, removing rocks, or defacing historical structures.

In conclusion, RV adventures within national parks offer an incredible opportunity to experience the beauty of nature while also enjoying the comforts of home on wheels. However, it comes with a responsibility to abide by rules and regulations that protect these natural wonders for current and future generations. Adherence to park hours, entrance fees, camping regulations, road and parking rules, outdoor activity guidelines, fire regulations, and pet rules is essential for a safe and enjoyable RV experience within national parks. By respecting these regulations, RV adventurers can help preserve these extraordinary landscapes while relishing the awe-inspiring beauty of America's national treasures.

Responsible wildlife viewing

One of the most thrilling aspects of RV adventure is encountering wildlife in their natural habitats. From majestic elk to elusive foxes and soaring eagles, the chance to witness these creatures up close is a privilege and a memorable part of the RV experience. However, with this privilege comes the responsibility of responsible wildlife viewing. This section will explore the importance of ethical wildlife viewing practices during RV adventures and how to minimize our impact on the animals and their ecosystems.

First and foremost, responsible wildlife viewing begins with respecting the animals and their space. Maintaining a secure and respectful distance from wildlife is crucial to avoid causing undue stress or disturbance. The particular distance may vary depending on the species and local regulations, but a general rule of thumb is to keep at least 100 yards (or more, if necessary) away from large mammals such as bears, bison, and moose. For smaller animals, birds, or marine life, it's essential to use binoculars or a camera with a telephoto lens to watch them from a safe distance. Close encounters can stress wildlife, disrupt their natural behaviors, and even lead to aggressive reactions, posing risks to both animals and humans.

Another vital aspect of responsible wildlife viewing is silence and patience. When approaching an area where wildlife may be present, minimize noise by turning off engines and keeping conversations hushed. Loud noises, such as slamming doors or shouting, can startle and frighten animals, causing them to flee or become agitated. While observing wildlife, remain patient and quiet, allowing the animals to acclimate to your presence. Sometimes, it may take a while for them to resume their normal activities, and patience often leads to more rewarding and natural behaviors to be observed.

Furthermore, avoid feeding wildlife under any circumstances. Offering food to wild animals can disrupt their natural diets and lead to dependency on human handouts. This can have detrimental consequences, including malnutrition, altered behavior, and aggression towards humans. Feeding wildlife in many national parks and protected areas is strictly prohibited and can result in fines or other penalties. Remember that human food is not suitable for wildlife and can harm their health.

Always comply to Leave No Trace principles to ensure your RV adventure leaves minimal impact on wildlife and their habitats. This includes packing out all trash, including food scraps, and disposing of waste properly. Additionally, be mindful of where you park your RV and set up camp. Choose established campsites when available, and avoid disturbing vegetation or disturbing sensitive habitats. Limit your environmental impact by following designated roads and staying on marked trails.

Responsible wildlife viewing also involves understanding and adhering to local regulations and guidelines. Many national parks and wildlife reserves have specific rules in place to secure both visitors and the animals. These regulations may include restrictions on where you can travel, using drones or other technology for wildlife observation, and using bait or calls to attract animals. Familiarize yourself with these rules before embarking on your RV adventure to ensure compliance and prevent accidental violations.

Lastly, consider the welfare of the animals when planning your RV itinerary. Some areas may be off-limits during breeding seasons, migrations, or critical times in an animal's life cycle. Research the best times to visit specific locations for wildlife viewing, and be mindful of any seasonal closures or restrictions in place to protect nesting birds or other vulnerable species.

In conclusion, responsible wildlife viewing is a crucial component of RV adventure, allowing us to appreciate the charm and diversity of the natural world while safeguarding the welfare of the animals and their habitats. By respecting the animals' space, maintaining silence and patience, avoiding feeding, following Leave No Trace principles, understanding local regulations, and considering the welfare of the animals, RV enthusiasts can enjoy ethical and rewarding wildlife encounters. These practices not only protect the wildlife but also contribute to the preservation of our natural heritage for generations to come. Responsible wildlife viewing enhances the RV experience by fostering a more profound connection with nature and promoting the conservation of our precious wildlife resources.

CHAPTER VI

RV Cooking and Meal Planning

Tips for cooking in an RV kitchen

Cooking in an RV kitchen can be both a delightful and challenging experience. While you may have limited space and resources compared to a traditional kitchen, preparing delicious and satisfying meals on the road is possible. In this section, we'll explore valuable tips and techniques to make the most of your RV kitchen and elevate your culinary adventures while traveling.

One of the keys to successful RV cooking is careful meal planning. Before hitting the road, create a menu that includes a variety of simple and flavorful dishes. Opt for recipes that require minimal equipment and ingredients, and consider prepping some items at home to save time and space in your RV kitchen. Having a meal plan not only ensures you have the necessary ingredients but also minimizes food waste.

RV kitchens have limited storage space, so selecting compact and stackable cookware is essential. Look for pots, pans, and utensils designed for RV living, as they are often designed with space-saving in mind. Non-stick cookware is ideal for easy cooking and cleanup. Additionally, consider investing in multi-purpose kitchen tools like a cast-iron skillet that can be used for various cooking methods.

Collapsible kitchen gadgets and accessories can be a lifesaver in an RV kitchen. Items like collapsible measuring cups, mixing bowls, and colanders save precious storage space when not in use. They are lightweight and easy to stow away, making them perfect for small kitchens.

Effective storage and organization are vital in an RV kitchen. Make use of cabinet organizers, hooks, and storage containers to maximize space and keep your kitchen tidy. Store items securely to prevent them from shifting during travel and potentially causing accidents.

One-pot and one-pan meals are ideal for RV cooking. These dishes minimize the number of dishes to wash and make the most of your limited kitchen space. Recipes like stir-fries, pasta dishes, and sheet pan dinners allow you to cook everything in a single container, saving time and effort.

If weather and campground regulations permit, outdoor cooking can expand your culinary options. An RV outdoor grill or portable camping stove can be used for grilling, frying, and other cooking methods. Cooking outside also helps keep the RV interior cooler during hot weather. Keep

your RV kitchen stocked with essential ingredients to simplify meal preparation. Staples like pasta, rice, canned vegetables, and non-perishable sauces can be the foundation for many meals. Also, carry a selection of herbs, spices, and condiments to improve the flavor of your dishes.

RV kitchens can become hot and stuffy when cooking, so ensure adequate ventilation. Use the RV's exhaust fan or open windows to let in fresh air and reduce cooking odors. Proper ventilation is essential for a comfortable cooking experience.

RV kitchens are equipped with propane stoves, so practicing safe cooking is crucial. Ensure that all propane connections are secure and regularly inspect for leaks. Always turn off the propane supply when not in use and store propane tanks properly. Follow all safety precautions outlined in your RV's user manual.

RV kitchens don't typically have large sinks or dishwashers, so minimizing cleanup is essential. Use disposable plates and utensils when feasible, and choose recipes that require minimal pots and pans. Assign a designated area for washing dishes and use biodegradable and environmentally friendly cleaning products.

In conclusion, cooking in an RV kitchen can be a rewarding as well as enjoyable experience with the right approach. By planning your meals, choosing compact cookware, using collapsible kitchen items, optimizing storage, mastering one-pot and one-pan meals, considering outdoor cooking, stocking essential ingredients, planning for proper ventilation, practicing safe cooking, and minimizing cleanup, you can make the most of your RV kitchen and create memorable culinary experiences while on the road. With a little creativity and adaptability, you can savor delicious meals and share them with loved ones, enhancing the overall joy of RV travel.

Delicious recipes for campfire cooking

Campfire cooking is integral to the RV adventure experience, offering a unique opportunity to savor flavorful meals while enjoying the great outdoors. A traditional kitchen can't quite capture the nostalgia and sense of being in nature that come with cooking over an open flame. In this section, we'll explore a selection of delicious campfire recipes that are perfect for your RV adventure, from breakfast to dinner and even dessert.

Begin your day with a hearty and satisfying campfire breakfast burrito. You'll need tortillas, eggs, diced bell peppers, onions, pre-cooked bacon or sausage, shredded cheese, and your favorite condiments to prepare. Start by cooking the sausage or bacon in a cast-iron skillet over the campfire until crispy. Remove it and set it aside. In the same skillet, sauté the diced vegetables until they become tender. Then, scramble the eggs and pour them to the skillet, cooking until they're fully set. Layer the tortillas with the cooked eggs, bacon or sausage, shredded cheese, and your preferred condiments. Wrap them up, and you can enjoy a portable, delicious breakfast by the campfire.

For a simple yet satisfying lunch, try campfire grilled cheese sandwiches. You'll need bread, butter, sliced cheese, and any optional fillings like ham, tomato, or avocado. Butter one side of each slice of bread. Sandwich a slice of cheese in between two pieces of bread, buttered sides out. Place the sandwich on a grill or over a campfire grate after wrapping it in aluminum foil. Cook until the cheese is melted and until the bread is golden brown, a few minutes on each side. Carefully unwrap the foil and enjoy your gooey, cheesy delight.

Foil packet meals are a favorite among campers for their simplicity and versatility. To make campfire foil packet meals, you can use various combinations of ingredients. One popular option is a chicken and vegetable foil packet. Start by placing a boneless chicken breast or thigh on a large sheet of aluminum foil. Add diced potatoes, carrots, bell peppers, and onions. Add your preferred herbs and spices along with salt and pepper for seasoning. Pour some olive oil over the foil, then fold it into a sealed packet. Cook the packet over the coals of the campfire for about 20 to 30 minutes, turning it from time to time, until the vegetables are soft and the chicken is cooked through. The end product is a full and tasty dinner that is prepared over a campfire.

No campfire experience is complete without s'mores, the classic and indulgent treat loved by all ages. You'll require graham crackers, marshmallows, and a chocolate bars to make s'mores. Roast marshmallows on skewers or sticks over the campfire until they are golden brown and gooey. Place a roasted marshmallow and a piece of chocolate between two graham crackers to make a sandwich. Allow the heat from the marshmallow melt the chocolate slightly, and enjoy the perfect blend of sweetness and crunch.

Before attempting any campfire cooking, it's essential to ensure safety. Check the campground or RV site's regulations regarding open fires and adhere to any restrictions or guidelines. Always keep a bucket of water, a fire extinguisher, and a shovel nearby for safety purposes. Use a designated fire ring or campfire grate when available; never leave the fire unattended.

When cooking over an open flame, use long utensils or skewers to keep a safe distance from the fire. It's also helpful to have oven mitts or heat-resistant gloves to handle hot cookware or foil packets. Consider using a windscreen or creating a barrier to protect the flames from gusts in windy conditions.

In conclusion, campfire cooking is a delightful and memorable aspect of RV adventures. Whether you're preparing breakfast burritos, grilled cheese sandwiches, foil packet meals, or s'mores, these recipes offer a taste of the outdoors and a connection to the camping tradition. Embrace the simplicity and rustic charm of campfire cooking while savoring delicious meals that enhance the overall enjoyment of your RV adventure.

Food storage and preservation

Embarking on an RV adventure is a thrilling way to explore the open road and immerse yourself in the beauty of nature. When it comes to food, however, RV travelers face unique challenges due to limited storage space, varying climates, and the need to plan for extended periods away from grocery stores. Proper food storage and preservation are crucial to ensure you have access to fresh, safe, and delicious meals throughout your journey. This section will explore essential tips and techniques for effectively storing and preserving food while on an RV adventure.

Choosing the right storage containers is the foundation of successful food storage in an RV. Opt for airtight and leak-proof containers that can keep food fresh and prevent spills during travel. Containers with multiple compartments are especially useful for organizing different food items. Additionally, consider using clear containers to identify contents and expiration dates quickly.

Vacuum sealing is a highly efficient method for extending the shelf life of perishable foods. Invest in a portable vacuum sealer that can remove air from bags and containers, preventing food from spoiling or becoming freezer-burned. Vacuum-sealed bags also save space in the RV refrigerator or freezer, permitting you to store more items efficiently.

Proper organization is key to maximizing the storage capacity of your RV refrigerator and freezer. Keep perishable items like dairy, meat, and vegetables in the fridge, and store frozen foods in the freezer. Use labeled bins or baskets to group similar items together, making it simpler to locate what you need. Regularly check the temperature settings to ensure your fridge and freezer maintain the appropriate levels.

If your RV is equipped with a dual-zone refrigerator, take advantage of it. Depending on your needs, these units have separate compartments that can function as a fridge or freezer. This flexibility permits you to adapt to changing storage requirements during your trip.

Dry food items, such as pasta, rice, cereal, and canned goods, can be stored in designated dry food containers or bins. These containers keep your dry goods organized, protect them from pests, and help maintain freshness. Label the containers to simply identify their contents.

To save space in your RV and reduce waste, consider removing excess packaging from items before storing them. Transfer items like cereal, snacks, and bulk goods into airtight containers or resealable bags. This conserves space and reduces the amount of trash you accumulate during your trip.

Meal planning is vital to food storage and preservation on an RV adventure. Plan your meals in advance and portion out ingredients accordingly. This reduces food waste and ensures you only carry what you need. Invest in reusable food storage bags for storing pre-measured portions of ingredients like marinades, sauces, or spices.

Maintaining a well-stocked pantry with non-perishable staples is essential for flexibility in your meal planning. Include items like canned vegetables, beans, pasta, rice, and condiments. Having a variety of pantry essentials on hand allows you to create meals even when you're away from grocery stores or fresh markets.

To prevent food from spoiling or expiring, practice the "first in, first out" (FIFO) method. Place newer items at the back of the storage areas and use older items first. Regularly check expiration dates and remove any expired or spoiled items promptly.

Understanding your RV's temperature and humidity levels is crucial for food storage. Keep temperature-sensitive items like dairy and meat in the coldest part of the refrigerator. To avoid moisture buildup in food storage containers, which can result in mold growth or spoiling, think about utilizing moisture-absorbing packets.

In conclusion, effective food storage and preservation are essential skills for a successful and enjoyable RV adventure. By investing in proper storage containers, using vacuum sealing, organizing your RV fridge and freezer, considering dual-zone refrigerators, utilizing dry food storage solutions, minimizing excess packaging, planning meals and portion sizes, keeping a well-stocked pantry, rotating your food supply, and being mindful of temperature and humidity, you can guarantee that your food keeps fresh as well as safe throughout your journey. These practices enhance the convenience and efficiency of RV cooking and contribute to a more sustainable and enjoyable travel experience.

CHAPTER VII

Exploring America's National Parks

Profiles of top National Parks (e.g., Yellowstone, Grand Canyon, Yosemite)

National parks across the United States offer RV enthusiasts unparalleled opportunities to connect with nature, witness breathtaking landscapes, and embark on unforgettable adventures. Among the most iconic and beloved national parks are Yellowstone, Grand Canyon, and Yosemite. In this section, we will explore these top national parks' unique characteristics and attractions, making them ideal destinations for RV adventures.

Yellowstone National Park:

Yellowstone, located primarily in Wyoming but extending into Montana and Idaho, is renowned for its stunning geothermal wonders, abundant wildlife, and dramatic landscapes. It was the first national park in the world, established in 1872, and covers over 2.2 million acres. RV travelers will be captivated by the park's hydrothermal features, including the iconic Old Faithful geyser, which erupts predictably with plumes of scalding water and steam.

The park is also home to a remarkable array of wildlife, like the grizzly bears, wolves, bison, elk, and numerous bird species. RV enthusiasts can explore the park's scenic roads, such as the Grand Loop Road, which connects the major attractions. Camping options in Yellowstone vary from developed campgrounds with RV hookups to more rustic sites, allowing travelers to immerse themselves in the park's natural beauty.

Grand Canyon National Park:

The Grand Canyon, located in Arizona, is one of Earth's most awe-inspiring natural wonders. This vast chasm, which spans 277 miles and descends more than a mile, was sculpted over millions of years by the Colorado River. RV adventurers can visit the North and South Rims of the Grand Canyon, each offering unique perspectives and experiences.

The South Rim, open year-round, is the more accessible of the two and features numerous viewpoints, hiking trails, and visitor centers. The North Rim, on the other hand, provides a quieter and more remote experience with fewer crowds. RV camping is available on both rims, but reservations are recommended, particularly during the peak season. Exploring the Grand Canyon by RV allows travelers to take their time marveling at the breathtaking vistas and hiking along the rim.

Yosemite National Park:

Yosemite, located in the Sierra Nevada of California, is renowned for its iconic waterfalls, granite cliffs, and lush valleys. Designated as a national park in 1890, Yosemite covers nearly 750,000 acres of pristine wilderness. RV enthusiasts are drawn to Yosemite for its diverse outdoor recreation opportunities and unparalleled scenic beauty.

One of the park's most famous landmarks is El Capitan, a colossal granite monolith that attracts rock climbers worldwide. With its towering waterfalls like Yosemite Falls and Bridalveil Fall, Yosemite Valley offers numerous hiking trails and viewpoints accessible by RV. The Glacier Point Road provides a stunning vista of the valley below. Yosemite also boasts several campgrounds that accommodate RVs, allowing travelers to experience the park's splendor while enjoying the comforts of their own vehicles.

While these national parks - Yellowstone, Grand Canyon, and Yosemite - stand out as top destinations for RV adventures, the United States offers a wealth of other incredible parks, each with its own unique features and attractions. Whether you're captivated by Yellowstone's geothermal wonders, the Grand Canyon's grandeur, or the natural beauty of Yosemite, an RV adventure in these national parks promises unforgettable experiences, opportunities for outdoor exploration, and a more profound connection to the wonders of the natural world. RV travelers have the privilege of immersing themselves in these pristine landscapes while enjoying the comforts and flexibility that RV living affords, making these parks ideal destinations for those seeking adventure, inspiration, and the beauty of America's national treasures.

Highlights and must-see attractions in each park

National parks in the United States offer RV enthusiasts a wealth of natural wonders and outdoor experiences. Exploring these parks in the comfort of your RV permits you to immerse yourself in the beauty of nature while having the convenience of home on wheels. Here, we will delve into the highlights and must-see attractions in three iconic national parks—Yellowstone, Grand Canyon, and Yosemite—making them exceptional destinations for RV adventures.

Yellowstone National Park:

Yellowstone, often referred to as the crown jewel of the national park system, boasts an array of captivating attractions. One of the park's most famous features is its geothermal wonders, including the iconic Old Faithful geyser. Witnessing Old Faithful's regular eruptions is a must-see spectacle, as scalding water and steam shoot into the sky with remarkable consistency.

Another highlight is the Grand Prismatic Spring, a massive, brilliantly colored hot spring that is the largest of its kind in the United States. The vibrant hues of the spring's microbial mats and mineral deposits are a sight to behold. RV adventurers can also explore the Yellowstone Grand Canyon, a striking canyon carved by the Yellowstone River, with two magnificent waterfalls—Upper Falls and Lower Falls.

Wildlife enthusiasts will be delighted by the park's diverse fauna, including grizzly bears, wolves, bison, elk, and eagles. Hayden Valley is a prime location for spotting bison and other wildlife. Lamar Valley, often called the "Serengeti of North America," offers excellent wolf-watching opportunities.

Camping in Yellowstone is a unique experience, with several campgrounds equipped for RVs. Be sure to make reservations well in advance, particularly during the busy summer season, to secure your spot in this remarkable wilderness.

Grand Canyon National Park:

The Grand Canyon's breathtaking vistas and unparalleled natural beauty make it a top destination for RV adventurers. The park offers two primary rims to explore—the South Rim and the North Rim—each with its own charm.

The South Rim, open year-round, is the more accessible of the two and features iconic viewpoints such as Mather Point and Yavapai Point. Take a leisurely stroll over the Rim Trail, which provides a never-ending view of the canyon. The South Rim also boasts visitor centers, restaurants, and various accommodations, making it convenient for RV travelers.

For a quieter and more remote experience, visit the North Rim, which is open from mid-May up to mid-October. The North Rim offers fewer crowds, cooler temperatures, and a different canyon perspective. Be sure to take in the view from Point Imperial, the highest point on the North Rim, and explore the trails that wind through the lush forests of the Kaibab Plateau.

RV camping is available on both rims, with numerous campgrounds equipped for various-sized RVs. It's best to make reservations in advance, especially during the busiest times of year.

Yosemite National Park:

Yosemite's breathtaking landscapes, iconic granite cliffs, and lush valleys have made it a beloved destination for RV adventurers. The park offers many must-see attractions, including the awe-inspiring El Capitan, a colossal granite monolith that lures rock climbers from around the world.

Yosemite Valley is home to some of the park's most famous waterfalls, including Yosemite Falls and Bridalveil Fall. Hike the Mist Trail to get up close to the powerful spray of Vernal Fall and Nevada Fall, or take in panoramic views of the valley from Glacier Point.

For a unique perspective of the park, explore the Giant Sequoias of Mariposa Grove, home to some of the world's largest trees. The Grizzly Giant and the California Tunnel Tree are must-see giants.

RV camping in Yosemite is a fantastic way to immerse yourself in the natural beauty of the park. Campgrounds like Upper Pines and Lower Pines offer RV-friendly sites, but reservations are highly recommended, particularly during the busy summer months.

While these national parks—Yellowstone, Grand Canyon, and Yosemite—hold distinct attractions and features, they all share the common thread of offering unforgettable RV adventure experiences. Whether you're marveling at the geothermal wonders of Yellowstone, gazing into the vastness of the Grand Canyon, or exploring the iconic landscapes of Yosemite, these parks invite you to connect with nature, embark on outdoor adventures, and make a lasting memories. RV travelers have the privilege of exploring these remarkable destinations with the freedom and comfort their vehicles provide, making these parks ideal choices for those seeking the ultimate road trip and natural beauty at its finest.

Recommended trails and activities

Embarking on an RV adventure offers the perfect opportunity to navigate the great outdoors and indulge in various outdoor activities. Whether you're a nature enthusiast, hiker, biker, or wildlife lover, there's something for everyone. In this section, we'll delve into a selection of recommended trails and activities for an RV adventure, showcasing the diverse experiences awaiting travelers.

One of the most common activities for RV travelers is hiking. All throughout the nation, there are a plethora of hiking trails, each with its own distinct charm and breathtaking scenery. From the rugged terrains of national parks like Zion and Bryce Canyon to the lush forests of the Appalachian Trail, there's a trail for hikers of all levels. Popular hikes include the Narrows in Zion National Park, the Angel's Landing Trail, the Pacific Crest Trail, and the Appalachian Trail.

For those who prefer exploring on two wheels, biking is a fantastic way to enjoy the great outdoors. Many RV parks and campgrounds offer bike-friendly trails, while some national parks, like Acadia in Maine, provide extensive networks of cycling paths. RV adventurers can also seek out dedicated mountain biking trails or embark on scenic road trips along iconic routes like the Blue Ridge Parkway.

Water-based activities offer another dimension to RV adventures. Kayaking and canoeing in serene lakes or rivers offer tranquil experiences, while white-water rafting on challenging rapids provides an adrenaline rush. The Colorado River through the Grand Canyon, the Boundary Waters Canoe Area Wilderness, and the Florida Keys are popular snorkeling and scuba diving locations.

Watching wildlife in their natural habitats is a captivating and educational experience. National parks such as Denali in Alaska, Everglades in Florida, and Custer State Park in South Dakota offer incredible opportunities to spot diverse animals, from grizzly bears and moose to alligators and bison. Consider using binoculars or joining ranger-led programs for expert guidance.

RV adventures often take travelers to remote and dark-sky areas, making them ideal for stargazing. Take out a pair of binoculars or a telescope, and head to designated dark-sky parks and reserves like Big Bend National Park, Joshua Tree National Park, or Cherry Springs State Park. Witnessing the night sky's splendor with minimal light pollution is an awe-inspiring experience.

For the thrill-seekers and climbing enthusiasts, RV adventures offer access to world-renowned climbing destinations. Consider scaling the granite walls of Yosemite's El Capitan, tackling the sandstone cliffs of Red Rock Canyon, or bouldering in Joshua Tree's surreal desert landscape. Safety is paramount, so be sure to follow recommended guidelines and consider hiring a local guide for assistance.

Birdwatching is a rewarding activity for RV travelers interested in avian species. Various national wildlife refuges and birding hotspots across the country, such as the Bosque del Apache National Wildlife Refuge in New Mexico or the Everglades in Florida, provide excellent opportunities to observe various bird species in their natural habitats. Bring along a field guide and binoculars to enhance your experience.

With the stunning landscapes and diverse wildlife that RV adventurers encounter, photography becomes integral to the journey. Capturing the perfect shot of a sunrise over the Grand Tetons, a bear cub in Yellowstone, or a cactus bloom in the Sonoran Desert can be immensely rewarding. Consider joining photography workshops or tours to enhance your skills and capture the beauty of the natural world.

In conclusion, an RV adventure is a gateway to a world of outdoor exploration and adventure. Whether you're hiking through rugged terrain, cycling along scenic paths, embarking on water adventures, observing wildlife in their natural habitats, stargazing under pristine night skies, climbing challenging rock formations, birdwatching in diverse ecosystems, or capturing the beauty of nature through photography, there's no shortage of activities to enjoy. The beauty of RV travel lies in the freedom to tailor your adventure to your interests and pace, making every journey a unique and memorable experience. So, hit the road, explore the diverse trails and activities the country offers, and create unforgettable memories on your RV adventure.

CHAPTER VIII

Hidden Gems and Lesser-Known Parks

Introducing readers to underrated National Parks

When it comes to RV adventures in the United States, well-known national parks like Yellowstone, Grand Canyon, and Yosemite often steal the spotlight. However, hidden gems await those seeking unique and less crowded experiences in underrated national parks. In this section, we'll introduce readers to some of these lesser- known treasures, showcasing the beauty, diversity, and solitude they offer for an unforgettable RV adventure.

1. Great Basin National Park, Nevada:

Great Basin National Park, tucked away in the eastern Nevada, is a sanctuary for those looking for peace and opportunities for stargazing. The park's vast desert landscapes, punctuated by ancient bristlecone pine forests and limestone caves, create a stark yet captivating environment. Wheeler Peak, the highest point in Nevada, offers panoramic views of the surrounding valleys, while Lehman Caves presents a subterranean wonderland of stalactites and stalagmites. RV adventurers can explore the park's hiking trails, enjoy dark-sky astronomy programs, and camp under the Milky Way in one of the park's campgrounds.

2. Congaree National Park, South Carolina:

Congaree National Park, which is located in the heart of South Carolina, is a hidden gem renowned for its immense old-growth floodplain forest. The park protects one of the largest and tallest deciduous hardwood forests in the eastern United States. RV travelers can explore the tranquil waters of Cedar Creek by canoe or kayak, hike along the boardwalks and trails through towering bald cypress trees, and birdwatch in this diverse ecosystem. The park's low visitation rates ensure a peaceful and immersive experience with nature.

3. North Cascades National Park, Washington:

Often overshadowed by its more famous counterparts in the Pacific Northwest, North Cascades National Park in Washington is a wilderness paradise waiting to be discovered. Known as the "American Alps," this park features rugged mountain peaks, pristine alpine lakes, and over 300 glaciers. RV adventurers can explore a network of hiking trails, including the iconic Cascade Pass Trail and the challenging but rewarding Sahale Arm Trail. Boating and fishing on the serene Ross Lake and Diablo Lake offer additional recreational opportunities. Despite its proximity to major cities like Seattle, North Cascades National Park remains a hidden gem for those seeking solitude in the mountains.

4. Guadalupe Mountains National Park, Texas:

Nestled in the rugged Chihuahuan Desert of West Texas, Guadalupe Mountains National Park boasts the highest peak in Texas, Guadalupe Peak. The park's dramatic landscapes feature rugged canyons, towering limestone cliffs, and unique desert flora. RV adventurers can hike to the summit of Guadalupe Peak for breathtaking views, explore hidden canyons, and marvel at the park's diverse wildlife. Guadalupe Mountains National Park's solitude and stark beauty offer a stark contrast to the bustling cities of Texas.

5. Isle Royale National Park, Michigan:

One of the least frequented national parks in the contiguous United States is Isle Royale National Park, which is situated in the crystal-clear waters of Lake Superior. This isolated island wilderness, only reachable by ferry or seaplane, has rocky hiking trails, pristine lakeshores, and a wealth of wildlife. RVers can kayak along the rocky coastline, explore the island's network of trails, and see wolves, moose, and other wildlife in their native environment. For those seeking for a genuine wilderness experience, Isle Royale is a hidden gem due to its remoteness and unspoiled beauty.

In conclusion, while Yellowstone, Grand Canyon, and Yosemite are rightfully celebrated as iconic national parks, these lesser-known treasures offer equally remarkable experiences for RV adventurers. Great Basin, Congaree, North Cascades, Guadalupe Mountains, and Isle Royale National Parks invite travelers to discover solitude, explore diverse ecosystems, and connect with nature more intimately. By venturing off the beaten path and navigating these underrated national parks, RV travelers can create unforgettable memories and gain a more profound appreciation for the diversity of America's natural landscapes.

Unique experiences in less crowded parks

While iconic national parks like Yellowstone and Grand Canyon draw millions of visitors each year, something is enchanting about exploring the lesser-known parks that offer unique experiences and the luxury of solitude. These less crowded parks allow RV adventurers to connect with nature on a deeper level, discover hidden treasures, as well as make memories that will last a lifetime. In this section, we'll delve into some of the most exceptional and less frequented national parks across the United States, showcasing their unique experiences for an unforgettable RV adventure.

1. Great Basin National Park, Nevada:

Great Basin National Park is an undiscovered treasure that beckons travelers looking for peace and amazing stargazing opportunities. It is tucked away in the center of eastern Nevada. The park's vast desert landscapes are punctuated by ancient bristlecone pine forests, limestone caves, and Wheeler Peak, the highest point in Nevada. Unique experiences abound here, from hiking the diverse trails that lead to breathtaking vistas to delving into the otherworldly beauty of Lehman Caves, adorned with stunning formations. What truly sets Great Basin apart is its designation as an International Dark Sky Park, offering some of the best stargazing in the country. RV adventurers can camp beneath a brilliant canopy of stars, participate in ranger-led astronomy programs, and witness the Milky Way in all its glory.

2. Congaree National Park, South Carolina:

Nestled in the floodplain of South Carolina's Congaree River, Congaree National Park is an underrated gem for nature enthusiasts and birdwatchers. The park's claim to fame is its incredible old-growth bottomland hardwood forest, and is one of the largest in the eastern United States. Unique experiences here include paddling Cedar Creek by canoe or kayak, where you'll glide beneath towering bald cypress trees draped with Spanish moss. Hiking along the boardwalks and trails offers encounters with centuries-old trees and diverse wildlife. The tranquility of Congaree National Park, with its lush greenery and serene waters, provides a peaceful escape from the hustle as well as bustle of our daily life.

3. North Cascades National Park, Washington:

North Cascades National Park, often overshadowed by nearby national parks, offers an extraordinary wilderness experience in the Pacific Northwest. This hidden gem is a haven for hikers, mountaineers, and nature lovers. RV adventurers can embark on unique experiences like hiking the breathtaking Cascade Pass Trail, which provides access to alpine meadows and jaw-dropping vistas. Sahale Arm Trail, though challenging, rewards hikers with unrivaled views of the surrounding peaks and glaciers. For a more leisurely experience, the park's serene lakes offer boating, fishing, and reflection opportunities. The pristine beauty and solitude of North Cascades National Park provide a sense of remoteness and serenity that's truly unparalleled.

4. Guadalupe Mountains National Park, Texas:

Located in the remote Chihuahuan Desert of West Texas, Guadalupe Mountains National Park boasts rugged canyons, towering limestone cliffs, and unique desert flora. This lesser-visited gem is home to the highest peak in Texas, Guadalupe Peak. RV travelers can experience the park's unique geological formations, including the stunning El Capitan and the colorful McKittrick Canyon. Hiking to the summit of Guadalupe Peak offers breathtaking panoramic scenes of the surrounding desert landscape. Birdwatchers will delight in the park's varied avian population, including peregrine falcons and golden eagles. Guadalupe Mountains National Park's tranquility and untouched beauty make it a haven for those seeking solitude and a connection with the desert wilderness.

5. Isle Royale National Park, Michigan:

One of the least visited national parks in the contiguous United States is Isle Royale National Park, which is tucked away in the crystal-clear waters of Lake Superior. This isolated island wilderness, only reachable by ferry or seaplane, provides RV travelers with an unforgettable experience. The park features rugged coastlines, dense forests, and abundant wildlife, including moose and wolves. Unique experiences here include exploring the network of hiking trails, kayaking along the rugged coastline, and observing the park's unique predator-prey relationship between wolves and moose. Isle Royale's isolation and untouched beauty make it a hidden gem for those looking for a true wilderness experience.

In conclusion, while the well-known national parks undoubtedly offer incredible experiences, these less crowded and underrated parks provide unique and intimate encounters with nature. Great Basin, Congaree, North Cascades, Guadalupe Mountains, and Isle Royale National Parks offer diverse landscapes, unparalleled solitude, and opportunities to create lasting memories. Exploring these hidden treasures allows RV adventurers to discover the beauty of America's less-visited natural wonders and forge a deeper connection with the wild landscapes that define our national park system.

Off-the-beaten-path adventures

Embarking on an RV adventure provides the freedom to explore popular destinations and off-the-beaten-path gems that offer unique and enriching travel experiences. While iconic national parks and well-known tourist attractions are undoubtedly captivating, some of the most memorable journeys can be found in lesser-known destinations. These hidden treasures allow RV travelers to immerse themselves in local culture, discover hidden gems, and forge a deeper connection with nature. This section will explore some off-the-beaten-path adventures that promise to deliver extraordinary and authentic experiences.

One of the joys of RV travel is the ability to uncover charming small towns and quaint villages that often remain unnoticed by mainstream tourism. These hidden gems provides a glimpse into local life, culture, and traditions. Travelers can savor regional cuisine at family-owned diners, partake in local festivals and farmers' markets, or engage in conversations with friendly locals. Exploring historic streets and appreciating the unique character of places like Jerome, Arizona, or Harmony, California, can lead to unexpected treasures and unforgettable experiences.

While highways and interstates offer convenience, the allure of scenic byways and backroads lies in the sense of adventure they provide. RV adventurers can chart their own course along these less-traveled routes, taking in breathtaking landscapes, encountering wildlife, and discovering hidden viewpoints. Think about driving the Extraterrestrial Highway in Nevada, the Million Dollar Highway in Colorado, or the Blue Ridge Parkway within North Carolina and Virginia. These routes offer spectacular scenery and opportunities for spontaneous detours and exploration.

Remote and dispersed camping is the answer for those seeking solitude and a more profound connection with nature. Many national forests, Bureau of Land Management (or BLM) lands, and wilderness areas offer dispersed camping opportunities, allowing RV travelers to camp in pristine and secluded settings. This off-the-grid experience may require water, waste disposal, and power generation self-sufficiency. However, the rewards include the serenity of being surrounded by natural beauty and the freedom to choose your campsite far from the crowds.

While national parks are renowned for their beauty and accessibility, state parks and lesser-known natural areas often offer equally stunning and less crowded experiences. These parks encompass diverse landscapes and provide various recreational activities, from hiking and birdwatching to boating and fishing. RV adventurers can explore hidden gems like Valley of Fire State Park in Nevada, Custer State Park in South Dakota, or Letchworth State Park in New York. These parks often feature well-maintained campgrounds with RV-friendly facilities, making them ideal destinations for a peaceful and natural retreat.

Engaging with local communities can be one of the most rewarding aspects of off-the-beaten-path RV travel. Attend local events, such as cultural festivals, art exhibitions, or historical reenactments, to gain insight into the region's heritage and traditions. Visit local markets, craft shops, and galleries to support local artisans and businesses. Strike up conversations with residents, and you may discover hidden gems recommended by locals, from secret hiking trails to hidden swimming holes.

Lastly, off-the-beaten-path adventures often involve outdoor activities that go beyond the ordinary. Consider trying unique pursuits such as rockhounding, where you can search for precious gems and minerals in designated areas, or ghost town exploration, where you can visit abandoned settlements and uncover their history. Seek out lesser-known hiking trails, kayak in remote lakes, or embark on wildlife safaris in areas that tourists do not overrun. These unconventional adventures offer a sense of discovery and excitement that can't be found in more popular destinations.

In conclusion, off-the-beaten-path RV adventures provide a rich tapestry of experiences that go beyond the expected. Exploring small towns, scenic byways, and remote camping spots, embracing lesser-known state parks and natural areas, connecting with local communities, and pursuing unconventional outdoor adventures allow RV travelers to create truly unique and unforgettable journeys. These off-the-beaten-path adventures offer solitude and authenticity and the chance to uncover hidden treasures and make meaningful connections with the people and places encountered along the way. By venturing off the beaten path, RV travelers can discover the true essence of their destination and create lasting memories that define the essence of travel itself.

CHAPTER IX

RV-Friendly Campgrounds

Listing RV-friendly campgrounds within National Parks

National parks are cherished treasures of natural beauty and biodiversity, offering visitors a chance to connect with the great outdoors and experience the splendor of unspoiled landscapes. For many, the allure of national parks extends beyond a day trip, leading them to embark on multi-day adventures by recreational vehicles (RVs). To cater to the requirements of RV enthusiasts, numerous national parks across the United States have designated RV-friendly campgrounds within their boundaries. These campgrounds provide the perfect opportunity for travelers to immerse themselves in the heart of nature while enjoying the comforts and conveniences of RV living. In this section, we will explore the concept of RV-friendly campgrounds within national parks, their significance, and some notable examples that beckon RVers to experience the beauty of nature firsthand.

The advent of RVs has revolutionized the way people experience national parks. RVs offer a unique combination of mobility and comfort, allowing visitors to explore the farthest reaches of these natural wonders while having all home necessities at their fingertips. However, not all campgrounds are suitable for RVs due to their size and specific requirements. Recognizing the growing popularity of RV travel, national parks have designated specific campgrounds as RV-friendly, ensuring that travelers with these vehicles can enjoy their stay without any hassles.

One significant aspect of RV-friendly campgrounds is their infrastructure. These campgrounds typically offer spacious pull-through or back-in sites that can accommodate RVs of varying sizes, including large motorhomes and trailers. In addition to ample space, they provide essential amenities such as electric hookups, water, and sewage disposal facilities. Some campgrounds even offer Wi-Fi access, allowing RVers to stay connected with the outside world while nestled in the heart of nature. These amenities make RV camping convenient and enjoyable for those who wish to explore national parks without sacrificing comfort.

The significance of RV-friendly campgrounds within national parks goes beyond convenience; they contribute to the preservation of these natural wonders. By providing designated areas for RVs, national parks can manage the impact of increased visitation and protect the fragile ecosystems that make these places special. Properly designed campgrounds ensure that RVers stay within designated areas, reducing the risk of environmental damage and overcrowding in sensitive areas. Additionally, the fees generated from RV campground reservations often go directly back into the park, supporting conservation efforts and infrastructure improvements.

One remarkable example of an RV-friendly campground within a national park is the "Furnace Creek Campground" in California's Death Valley National Park. Nestled in the heart of the world's hottest and driest desert, this campground offers RV sites with full hookups and stunning views of the surrounding desert landscape. RVers can explore the unique geologic formations, vibrant desert wildflowers, and starry night skies while enjoying the comfort of their RVs. Another notable option is the "Mather Campground" in Arizona's Grand Canyon National

Park, offering RV sites within easy reach of the Grand Canyon's awe-inspiring vistas.

Yellowstone National Park in Wyoming, known for its geothermal wonders and abundant wildlife, also features RV-friendly campgrounds such as the "Madison Campground" and "Fishing Bridge RV Park." These campgrounds allow RVers to witness the park's iconic geysers and hot springs while staying close to the park's main attractions.

In conclusion, RV-friendly campgrounds within national parks are a boon to both travelers and the parks themselves. They offer a unique opportunity for RV enthusiasts to experience the natural wonders of these protected areas while enjoying the comforts of their vehicles. These campgrounds also play a crucial role in preserving the environment by managing the impact of increased visitation. As more people discover the joys of RV travel, the popularity of RV-friendly campgrounds within national parks is likely to continue to grow, ensuring that generations to come can experience the magic of these natural wonders while protecting them for the future.

Booking strategies and tips for securing a spot

Embarking on an RV adventure is an exciting way to explore the great outdoors and experience the freedom of the open road. However, as the popularity of RV travel has surged in recent years, so has the demand for RV campsites and campgrounds. Securing a spot for your RV adventure can sometimes be challenging, particularly during peak travel seasons. To help you navigate this process successfully, this section will delve into various booking strategies and tips that will make sure you find the perfect spot for your RV journey.

First and foremost, planning ahead is key when it comes to booking RV campsites. Many popular campgrounds within national parks, state parks, and private RV parks fill up quickly, sometimes months in advance. Therefore, starting your booking process as early as possible is advisable. Whether you're planning a trip during the peak summer season or a quieter off-season excursion, reserving your spot well in advance can help you secure the dates and locations you desire.

One effective strategy is to utilize online reservation systems. Many campgrounds and RV parks now offer online booking platforms, allowing you to browse available dates and select your preferred site. These systems often provide detailed information about each site, including its size, amenities, and proximity to recreational activities. By booking online, you can also avoid the disappointment of arriving at a campground only to find it fully occupied.

If you're planning to visit a highly sought-after destination, consider being flexible with your travel dates. Adjusting your schedule by a few days or weeks can significantly affect availability. For example, visiting a national park during the shoulder season (known as spring or fall) instead of the peak summer months may increase your chances of securing a campsite without the crowds.

Another valuable tip is to explore alternative campgrounds in the vicinity of your desired destination. While popular national parks may be your primary goal, nearby state parks, national forests, or private campgrounds can offer equally memorable experiences. These alternatives often have fewer visitors and more availability, making them excellent options for RVers looking for a tranquil escape.

When planning your RV adventure, it's essential to conduct thorough research. To learn more and read reviews from other RV enthusiasts, use online resources, RV travel forums, and campground review websites. These resources can offer insightful information about the standard of campgrounds, the state of the facilities, and any potential difficulties you might run into. By compiling this data, you can make well-informed decisions and steer clear of unpleasant surprises.

Additionally, consider joining RV clubs or memberships that offer exclusive access to campgrounds and discounted rates. Organizations like Good Sam Club and Passport America provide RVers with access to a network of affiliated campgrounds, special discounts, and priority reservations. These memberships can be specifically advantageous for frequent RV travelers seeking consistent and affordable camping options.

Lastly, remain flexible and adaptable in your RV adventure planning. Even with the best strategies and tips, unexpected changes in your travel itinerary may occur. Having backup plans, such as knowing nearby campgrounds or boondocking options, can save you from unnecessary stress and ensure that your RV adventure remains enjoyable and memorable.

In conclusion, booking strategies and tips are crucial in securing a spot for an RV adventure, especially in today's competitive camping landscape. By planning ahead, utilizing online reservation systems, being flexible with travel dates, exploring alternative campgrounds, conducting research, and considering RV club memberships, you can enhance your chances of securing the ideal campsite for your journey. Remember that flexibility and adaptability are essential attributes for RVers, ensuring that you can embrace the spontaneity of the road while still enjoying the comforts of a well-planned RV adventure.

Campground amenities and facilities

When embarking on an RV adventure, one of the essential factors that can greatly improve your experience is the campground selection. Campgrounds come in various shapes and sizes, and their range of amenities and facilities can vary widely. Choosing the right campground that aligns with your preferences and needs can make your RV journey more comfortable, enjoyable, and memorable. In this section, we will explore the diverse array of campground amenities and facilities that are essential for an enriching RV adventure.

Electrical hookups are one of the most fundamental amenities to consider when selecting a campground for your RV adventure. Many RVs rely on electricity to power appliances, lighting, and heating or cooling systems. Campgrounds typically offer different levels of electrical hookups, such as 30-amp or 50-amp service, to accommodate various types of RVs. Access to electrical hookups ensures you can maintain a comfortable and functional living space within your RV throughout your stay.

Water hookups and sanitation facilities are equally vital amenities. Most campgrounds provide freshwater hookups at each site, allowing you to easily fill your RV's freshwater tank. Additionally, having access to a sewage dump station or a full hookup site with sewer connections is crucial for proper waste disposal. These amenities ensure that you can maintain sanitary conditions within your RV without the need for frequent trips to a nearby dump station.

A popular feature in many modern campgrounds is Wi-Fi access. While some RV travelers seek a complete escape from the digital world, others may need to stay connected for work, communication, or entertainment. Campgrounds with reliable Wi-Fi connections allow you to enjoy the conveniences of the internet while still savoring the natural beauty of your surroundings.

For those who enjoy recreational activities, amenities such as hot tubs, swimming pools, and fitness centers can be a welcomed addition to a campground. These facilities provide relaxation, exercise, and social interaction opportunities with fellow campers. In particular, swimming pools and hot tubs can be delightful during warm summer days or chilly evenings.

Campgrounds with playgrounds, game rooms, and planned activities can keep everyone entertained if you're traveling with family or children. These amenities can foster a sense of community and provide a fun and enriching experience for children, allowing parents to relax as well as unwind while their kids are engaged in supervised activities.

Many campgrounds also offer communal gathering spaces, such as picnic areas, fire pits, and barbecue grills. These areas encourage campers to socialize, share meals, and enjoy the outdoors together. Gathering around a campfire for s'mores and storytelling is a cherished tradition for many RV enthusiasts.

Nature enthusiasts will appreciate campgrounds that provide easy access to hiking trails, fishing ponds or streams, and birdwatching opportunities. The proximity of these amenities allows you to immerse yourself in the area's natural beauty, providing endless opportunities for exploration and outdoor adventures.

Safety and security should not be overlooked when choosing a campground. Look for campgrounds implementing security measures, such as gated entrances, well-lit pathways, and on-site staff or hosts. Feeling secure in your surroundings will allow you to relax and enjoy your RV adventure without worry.

In conclusion, the amenities and facilities offered by campgrounds play a pivotal role in shaping the overall experience of your RV adventure. Electrical and water hookups, sewage disposal options, Wi-Fi access, and recreational facilities are all factors to consider when selecting a campground that suits your preferences and needs. Whether you seek a tranquil escape in nature, a family-friendly environment, or opportunities for social interaction, there is a campground out there with the amenities and facilities to make your RV adventure genuinely memorable. By carefully choosing a campground that aligns with your desires, you can maximize the comfort and enjoyment of your RV journey while creating lasting memories along the way.

CHAPTER X

RV Life on the Road

Coping with long drives

An RV adventure offers the allure of freedom, exploration, and the open road. However, it's essential to recognize that RV travel often entails long drives between destinations, and coping with these extended periods on the road is crucial to enjoying your journey. From planning your route and managing fatigue to staying entertained and comfortable, there are various strategies and considerations to make long drives a manageable and enjoyable aspect of your RV adventure.

First and foremost, careful route planning is essential. Before embarking on your journey, use navigation apps or GPS devices designed for RV travel to map out your route. These tools can help you identify RV-friendly roads, low-clearance obstacles, and the locations of campgrounds and rest stops along your way. Planning your route in advance permits you to avoid unexpected detours and ensures a smoother, stress-free journey.

Managing fatigue is paramount during long drives. RVs provide a comfortable living space but are not designed for non-stop driving. It's vital to schedule regular rest breaks to rest, stretch, and refresh. Aim to stop every two to three hours, or as needed, to combat driver fatigue. During these breaks, take the opportunity to walk around, hydrate, and have a snack. If you're traveling with a partner or co-driver, consider taking turns behind the wheel to share the driving responsibilities and stay alert.

Staying entertained and engaged during long drives is essential for keeping spirits high. Create a playlist of your favorite podcasts, music, or audiobooks to keep the atmosphere enjoyable. Additionally, consider in-vehicle entertainment options for passengers like DVDs, streaming services, or board games. Engaging activities can make the journey more enjoyable for everyone on board, especially during extended drives.

Food and hydration are crucial elements to consider while coping with long drives. Plan your meals and snacks in advance, packing a cooler with various easy-to-eat foods and beverages. Avoid heavy, greasy foods that can induce drowsiness. Opt for light, nutritious options that provide sustained energy and keep you alert. Staying hydrated is equally important, as dehydration can lead to fatigue and reduced concentration. Carry a supply of water and drink regularly throughout the journey.

Comfort is key to managing long drives in an RV. Ensure that your driving seat and posture are ergonomically sound to reduce the risk of discomfort or back pain. Adjust your seat, steering wheel, and mirrors to your liking, and use seat cushions or lumbar supports if necessary. Dress in comfortable clothing suitable for long periods of sitting, and consider investing in a good-quality RV mattress for a restful sleep at night.

Navigating inclement weather is another challenge during long drives. Be prepared for adverse weather conditions by checking weather forecasts before hitting the road. If you encounter rain, snow, or high winds, adjust your driving speed accordingly, maintain a safe following distance, and exercise caution when navigating curves or hills. Carry essential emergency supplies such as a first-aid kit, flashlight, and roadside assistance tools in case of unexpected situations.

Long drives can become boring if you don't make enjoyable pit stops along the way. These stops also present opportunities for exploration. Research interesting landmarks, scenic overlooks, or quirky roadside attractions along your route. These stops can add a touch of excitement and novelty to your RV adventure, making the journey itself a memorable part of the experience.

Lastly, maintaining a positive mindset is vital when coping with long drives. Embrace the journey as an integral part of your RV adventure, not just a means to an end. Take in the changing landscapes, appreciate the beauty of the open road, and savor the moments of togetherness with your travel companions. A positive attitude can transform long drives into cherished memories of your RV adventure.

In conclusion, while long drives are an inherent aspect of RV travel, they need not be a daunting or unpleasant part of your adventure. Careful planning, fatigue management, entertainment options, proper nutrition and hydration, comfort considerations, weather awareness, enjoyable pit stops, and a positive mindset all play essential roles in coping with long drives. By implementing these strategies and staying flexible in your approach, you can turn your RV journey into a road trip filled with discovery, relaxation, and lasting memories.

Managing waste and utilities

An RV adventure allows you to experience the freedom of the open road while enjoying the comforts of home. However, to fully enjoy this nomadic lifestyle, it's essential to understand how to manage waste and utilities effectively. Whether it's handling freshwater and wastewater, managing propane and electricity, or maintaining your RV's systems, mastering these aspects is key to a successful and enjoyable RV adventure. This section will delve into the various aspects of managing waste and utilities for an RV adventure, offering insights and tips for a smooth journey.

Freshwater management is the first step in your RV adventure. Most RVs have a freshwater tank that provides potable water for drinking, cooking, and bathing. Before hitting the road, ensure your tank is clean and filled to the desired level. Many campgrounds offer water hookups, allowing you to replenish your freshwater supply as needed. To conserve water during your trip, consider using water-saving fixtures and taking shorter showers. Additionally, it's essential to carry a water filtration system to ensure the quality of the water you consume. On the flip side, managing wastewater is equally crucial. RVs have two types of wastewater tanks: gray water and black water. Gray water is generated from sinks, showers, and washing machines, while black water contains human waste from the toilet. To maintain these tanks, use RV-safe biodegradable soaps and chemicals to minimize odors and prevent clogs. Empty your tanks at designated dump stations or full-hookup campsites to ensure proper disposal. Practice responsible waste disposal, and never dump wastewater on the ground or in unauthorized locations to protect the environment.

Propane is an essential utility for cooking, heating, and operating appliances in many RVs. Proper management of your propane supply is critical to ensure a continuous fuel source. Check your propane levels regularly using the built-in gauge or a separate propane level indicator. Always have a backup propane tank on hand in case your primary tank runs out during your journey. To avoid accidents, ensure your propane system is leak-free, and turn off the propane supply when not in use or while driving.

Electricity is another utility that requires careful management during an RV adventure. RVs have electrical systems powered by batteries, generators, or shore power (plugging into a campground's electrical hookup). Monitor your battery levels to prevent over-discharging, which can damage your batteries. Carry a generator or solar panels to recharge your batteries when camping off-grid. When connected to shore power, use surge protectors to safeguard your RV's electrical system from power surges. Always follow safety guidelines when employing electrical appliances to prevent overloading circuits and minimize the risk of fires.

Proper maintenance of your RV's systems and appliances is essential to ensure their reliability throughout your adventure. Conduct routine checks of your RV's plumbing, electrical, and propane systems to promptly identify and address any issues. Regularly clean and maintain your RV's appliances, such as the refrigerator, stove, and water heater, to extend their lifespan and efficiency. Having a basic toolkit and spare parts on hand can be a lifesaver when minor repairs are needed while on the road.

When it comes to managing waste and utilities, environmentally conscious practices should be a priority. Minimize water and energy consumption by adopting eco-friendly habits like turning off the lights and appliances when not in use, utilizing LED bulbs, and reducing waste by recycling and composting. Choose campgrounds and dump stations that prioritize sustainability and responsible waste disposal.

In conclusion, effective management of waste and utilities is essential for a successful and enjoyable RV adventure. This includes maintaining your freshwater and wastewater systems, responsibly managing propane and electricity, and regularly maintaining your RV's systems and appliances. By following best practices, adopting eco-friendly habits, and staying vigilant about conserving resources, you can ensure that your RV adventure is comfortable and environmentally responsible. Mastering these aspects of RV living allows you to embrace the freedom of the open road fully and create lasting memories during your nomadic journey.

Staying connected on the road

In today's digital age, staying connected while embarking on an RV adventure has become a top priority for many travelers. Whether you need to work remotely, keep in touch with loved ones, or access essential information, maintaining connectivity on the road is essential. Fortunately, with the advancement of technology and the availability of various connectivity options, RVers can now enjoy the best of both worlds: the freedom of the open road and the ability to stay connected. This section will explore the strategies, tools, and tips for staying connected on the road during an RV adventure.

One of the primary considerations for staying connected is choosing the right cellular plan. Most RVers rely on cellular networks to access the internet, make calls, and send messages. To ensure reliable connectivity, research and select a cellular plan that offers good coverage in the areas you plan to travel. Consider carriers with nationwide coverage and check online coverage maps for your route. Additionally, choose a plan with sufficient data allowance to meet your needs, especially if you plan to stream videos or work online.

To boost your cellular signal, invest in a cellular signal booster. These devices amplify weak signals, helping you stay connected even in remote or low-signal areas. A quality signal booster can significantly improve your internet speed and call quality, enhancing your overall connectivity experience. When using a signal booster, position it properly inside your RV to maximize its effectiveness.

Mobile hotspots are another valuable tool for maintaining connectivity on the road. Many cellular providers offer mobile hotspot devices that create a Wi-Fi network in your RV. You can simultaneously connect numerous devices, including laptops, tablets, and smartphones, to the internet with a mobile hotspot. It offers you convenience and flexibility by letting you work, stream, or browse from a variety of devices inside your RV.

Wi-Fi can be found at many campgrounds and RV parks, but its quality can vary widely. To enhance your Wi-Fi experience, consider carrying a Wi-Fi extender or booster. These devices can increase the range and strength of a campground's Wi-Fi signal, making it more accessible within your RV. Additionally, some campgrounds offer premium Wi-Fi options for faster and more reliable connections, which may be worth the investment if you depend on internet access for work or entertainment.

Satellite internet is an option for RVers who frequently venture into remote areas with restricted cellular coverage. Although satellite internet can be more expensive and less convenient than cellular options, it provides reliable connectivity in areas where other options may not work. To access satellite internet, you'll need a satellite dish installed on your RV and a service plan from a satellite internet provider.

Staying connected also involves managing your data usage efficiently. Be mindful of data-heavy activities such as streaming high-definition videos or downloading large files, as these can quickly deplete your data allowance. Optimize your devices and apps to reduce data consumption by adjusting settings to lower video quality, enabling data-saving features, and using offline modes whenever possible.

When traveling internationally, ensure that your cellular plan supports international roaming or purchase a local SIM card in your destination country for cost-effective connectivity. International mobile hotspot devices can also provide a convenient solution for staying connected while abroad.

In conclusion, staying connected on the road during an RV adventure is entirely achievable with the right strategies and tools. Choose a reliable cellular plan with good coverage, invest in a signal booster, use mobile hotspots and Wi-Fi extenders, and consider satellite internet when necessary. Use your data wisely and be prepared for international travel with appropriate connectivity solutions. By implementing these strategies and staying updated about the latest technological advancements, RVers can enjoy the freedom of the open road while also staying connected to work, family, and the digital world. Staying connected allows you to make the most of your RV adventure while maintaining the conveniences of modern life.

CHAPTER XI

Capturing the Moment

Photography and videography tips

Capturing the beauty and memories of your RV adventure through photography and videography is a wonderful way to relive and share your journey with others. With the ever-improving quality of smartphone cameras and the availability of compact, high-quality cameras and camcorders, creating stunning visuals has become even more accessible. This section will explore valuable photography and videography tips to help you document your RV adventure effectively and artistically.

Before you embark on your RV adventure, take some time to plan your shots. Research your destinations and identify key locations, landmarks, and natural wonders you want to capture. Consider the best times of day for photography, like the golden hours of sunrise and sunset when the lighting is soft and warm. Planning your shots in advance allows you to maximize your time and opportunities.

While high-end cameras and lenses can produce exceptional results, you don't need expensive equipment to capture memorable moments. Modern smartphones often feature advanced camera capabilities, including multiple lenses, manual settings, and various shooting modes. If you choose to invest in a dedicated camera, consider a lightweight mirrorless camera or a compact DSLR for portability and versatility.

Composition is key to creating compelling photographs and videos. Familiarize yourself with basic composition principles such as the rule of thirds, leading lines, as well as framing. Experiment with diverse angles and perspectives to add depth as well as interest to your shots. Don't be afraid to get creative and try unconventional framing or composition techniques.

Lighting is one of the most critical elements in photography and videography. Whenever possible, rely on natural light, especially during the golden hours mentioned earlier. Harsh midday sunlight can lead to harsh shadows and blown-out highlights, so if you must shoot during these times, consider finding shade or using diffusers to soften the light.

While wide-angle shots are great for capturing landscapes and scenery, don't forget to zoom in and capture details that tell a story. Close-up shots of flora, fauna, unique textures, or personal mementos can add depth and variety to your visual storytelling.

Think of your RV adventure as a narrative. Document the places you visit, the individuals you meet, the challenges you overcome, and the emotions you experience along the way. Include personal anecdotes and reflections in your videos or photo captions to create a richer storytelling experience.

To ensure smooth and steady footage, invest in stabilizing equipment. Tripods, gimbals, or monopods can help eliminate shaky shots, making your videos more professional and enjoyable to watch. Many smartphones and cameras also have built-in stabilization features that you can activate.

Good audio quality is crucial for videography. Invest in an external microphone if your camera or smartphone allows for one. A directional microphone can help minimize background noise and capture clear, focused audio, enhancing the overall quality of your videos.

While on the road, make it a habit to regularly back up your photos and videos to a protected location. Consider using external hard drives, cloud storage, or portable backup devices to ensure your precious memories are safe in case of equipment failure or loss.

Photography and videography are skills that improve with practice. Experiment with different settings, techniques, and styles to find your unique voice as a visual storyteller. Don't be discouraged by mistakes; they often lead to valuable learning experiences.

In conclusion, documenting your RV adventure through photography and videography allows you to relive and share your experiences with others while creating lasting memories. You can enhance the caliber of your visual content by organizing your shots, becoming an expert in composition, utilizing natural light, catching details, and putting a strong emphasis on storytelling. Invest in the right gear, stabilize your shots, capture high-quality audio, and don't forget to back up your work to safeguard your memories. Above all, enjoy yourself and the creative process while you set out on your RV adventure with a camera in hand.

Keeping a travel journal

The thrill of embarking on an RV adventure is a dream for many. It's a chance to explore the open road, discover new places, and create lasting memories. One valuable tool that can enhance this experience is a travel journal. Keeping a travel journal during an RV adventure allows you to capture the essence of your journey, preserve precious memories, and gain insights into your travels that may otherwise be forgotten. In this section, we will explore the benefits of keeping a travel journal for an RV adventure and provide tips on creating and maintaining one effectively.

To begin with, a travel journal records your journey's highlights, whether it's visiting breathtaking national parks, meeting interesting people, or enjoying local cuisine. As you jot down your experiences, you capture the moment's essence, making it easier to relive them later. Unlike photos or videos, which visually represent your journey, a journal allows you to delve deeper into your emotions and thoughts at each stage of your adventure. It helps you remember what you saw and how you felt.

Furthermore, a travel journal can be an invaluable source of information for future trips. When you document details such as campground reviews, road conditions, and local attractions, you create a personalized guidebook that can be referred to when planning future RV adventures. When you return to a favorite destination or recommend it to others, this can save you time and effort. Additionally, it can be a helpful resource for fellow travelers seeking recommendations and advice.

In addition to the practical benefits, keeping a travel journal can also be a profoundly fulfilling and reflective experience. Writing about your journey allows you to connect with your surroundings and the people you encounter on a deeper level. You may find yourself paying more attention to the small details and nuances of each place you visit, fostering a sense of mindfulness and gratitude. Moreover, journaling can be a therapeutic outlet for processing your thoughts and emotions, especially during challenging or introspective moments of your adventure.

Now that we have discussed the importance of keeping a travel journal during an RV adventure, let's explore some tips on creating and maintaining one effectively. Firstly, choose a journal that suits your preferences. It could be a traditional paper notebook, a digital journaling app, or a combination of both. Consider factors including convenience, ease of use, and your personal writing style. Whatever medium you choose, make sure it's easily accessible during your journey.

Secondly, establish a routine for journaling. Find a time of day that works best for you, whether it's in the morning as you sip coffee by your RV, during a peaceful afternoon break, or in the evening as you unwind from the day's adventures. Consistency is key to maintaining your travel journal. Allocate a specific period of time to contemplate your encounters and record your ideas and insights.

Additionally, don't feel pressured to write lengthy entries every day. Even a few paragraphs or bullet points can suffice to capture the essence of your day. Include details like the date, location, weather, and any notable events or encounters. Remember, the goal is to document your journey in a way that resonates with you, so there are no strict rules to follow.

Lastly, get creative with your journaling. Incorporate sketches, doodles, photographs, or mementos like ticket stubs and postcards to add a visual dimension to your entries. Experiment with different writing styles like narrative storytelling, descriptive prose, or reflective essays. Your travel journal is a personal space for self-expression, so let your creativity flow.

In conclusion, keeping a travel journal for an RV adventure is a rewarding and enriching practice. It allows you to preserve cherished memories, create a valuable resource for future trips, and engage with your surroundings on a deeper level. By following the tips mentioned above and making journaling a part of your RV journey, you'll find that it enhances your travel experience in countless ways, making your adventures more memorable and meaningful. So, don't forget to pack a journal on your next RV adventure and start capturing the magic of the open road.

Creating memorable travel stories

Embarking on an RV adventure is an opportunity to escape the ordinary and navigate the extraordinary. Whether you're traversing scenic highways, camping in picturesque locations, or encountering new cultures, an RV journey offers a wealth of experiences worth sharing. Crafting memorable travel stories from these adventures preserves your precious memories and allows you to inspire others and relive your journey. In this section, we will delve into the art of creating unforgettable travel stories for an RV adventure, exploring the key elements that make these tales come alive.

To begin with, every compelling travel story starts with a captivating narrative. While it's essential to recount the events and places you visited during your RV adventure, infusing your storytelling with a personal touch is equally crucial. Share your emotions, thoughts, and reactions to the places and experiences you encountered. Describe the awe-inspiring landscapes that took your breath away, the delicious local cuisines that tantalized your taste buds, and the people whose stories left a lasting impression. By adding your unique perspective, you create a connection with your readers, allowing them to see the world through your eyes.

Additionally, travel stories are enriched when they explore the transformative power of the journey. Share how your RV adventure changed you, whether through personal growth, newfound perspectives, or unexpected challenges. Highlight the lessons learned and the moments of self-discovery that occurred along the way. These reflections add depth to your story, making it not just a travelogue but a meaningful exploration of the human experience.

Another essential element of crafting memorable travel stories is the art of vivid description. Paint a vivid picture with your words, permitting your readers to immerse themselves in your journey's sights, sounds, and sensations. Describe the lush green forests, the crystal-clear mountain streams, the bustling city streets, and the starry nights by the campfire. Use sensory details to transport your audience to the very places you visited, evoking a sense of wanderlust and adventure.

Photographs can also be significant in enhancing your travel stories. While words create mental images, photos provide a visual anchor, allowing readers to see the beauty of the places you explored and the smiles of the people you met. Incorporate images strategically within your narrative to complement your descriptions and add a visual dimension to your storytelling. A well-chosen photograph can evoke emotions and memories like no words can.

Furthermore, travel stories are often brought to life by including memorable anecdotes and encounters. Share the quirky roadside attractions you stumbled upon, the heartwarming interactions with fellow travelers, and the unexpected detours that turned into unforgettable adventures. These anecdotes not only entertain but also provide a glimpse into the serendipitous nature of RV travel, where the unplanned moments often become the most cherished.

Moreover, structure and organization are crucial aspects of crafting compelling travel stories. Consider the beginning, middle, and end of your narrative. Start with a captivating hook that draws readers in, provides context about your RV adventure, and gradually builds the plot, culminating in a satisfying conclusion. Use transitions to guide your readers seamlessly from one part of the journey to the next, creating a cohesive and engaging narrative flow.

In conclusion, creating memorable travel stories for an RV adventure is an art that combines narrative skill, personal reflection, vivid description, and the power of visuals. By infusing your storytelling with your unique perspective, sharing the transformative aspects of your journey, and using sensory details and photographs to transport your readers, you can craft tales that not only preserve your memories but also inspire and captivate your audience. So, as you embark on your next RV adventure, remember to document it in a way that brings your experiences to life, turning your journey into unforgettable stories that will be cherished for years to come.

CHAPTER XII

Staying Safe in the Wilderness

Navigating wildlife encounters

One of the greatest appeals of an RV adventure is the opportunity to immerse oneself in the beauty and serenity of nature. As you traverse diverse landscapes, you may encounter various wildlife, from majestic deer and playful squirrels to awe-inspiring bears and elusive mountain lions. While these encounters can be exhilarating and provide a deeper connection to the natural world, they also come with a set of challenges and responsibilities. This section will explore the importance of navigating wildlife encounters responsibly and offer guidance on how to do so during your RV adventure.

First and foremost, it's essential to approach wildlife encounters with the utmost respect for the creatures and their habitats. While getting close for a better view or a perfect photograph is tempting, remember that these animals are wild and unpredictable. Maintain a safe distance, as specified by park regulations and guidelines, and use binoculars or zoom lenses for a closer look. Avoid disturbing the animals; sudden movements or loud noises can cause stress or provoke defensive behaviors.

Furthermore, it's crucial to keep your presence as unobtrusive as possible. Wildlife encounters are best enjoyed when you are a silent observer. Turn off radios, refrain from playing music loudly, and keep conversations to a minimum when you are in areas known for wildlife sightings. This allows you to blend into the natural surroundings and increases your chances of witnessing animals in their natural behaviors.

Safety is paramount when navigating wildlife encounters during an RV adventure. Depending on your destination, you may meet animals that can harm you and themselves. For example, bears are known to be attracted to food, so it's essential to store your food properly and follow bear-proofing guidelines in areas where bears are present. Additionally, learn about the specific wildlife in the region you are visiting and understand their behaviors, so you can react appropriately if you encounter them. For example, if you come across a moose, keeping a significant distance is best, as they can be unpredictable and territorial.

Another important aspect of responsible wildlife encounters is understanding the effect of human activity on the environment. Campfires, litter, and disturbances can harm wildlife habitats and disrupt their natural behaviors. Follow the Leave No Trace principles by using established campsites, packing out all trash, and minimizing your impact on the ecosystem. By practicing responsible camping and hiking, you help preserve the natural environment for both the wildlife and future generations of adventurers.

Moreover, it's crucial to be aware of the laws and regulations regarding wildlife encounters in the areas you visit. Many national parks and protected areas have specific guidelines in place to ensure the safety of both visitors and wildlife. Familiarize yourself with these rules before embarking on your RV adventure, and adhere to them diligently. These regulations are designed to protect both you and the animals and are essential for preserving these unique environments.

In addition to practicing responsible behavior, consider the welfare of the wildlife during your encounters. Don't feed wild animals because it can make them reliant on human food and interfere with their natural foraging habits. Feeding wildlife can also harm their health and increase the risk of disease transmission. Instead, observe them from a distance and let them find their own food sources.

Finally, share your experiences and knowledge of responsible wildlife encounters with fellow travelers. Educate others about respecting wildlife and their habitats and encourage them to follow ethical practices during their RV adventures. By promoting responsible behavior and conservation awareness, we can collectively contribute to protecting these precious natural wonders.

In conclusion, wildlife encounters during an RV adventure can be a thrilling as well as enriching experience, offering a glimpse into the charm and diversity of the natural world. However, as adventurers, we are responsible for approaching these encounters with respect, safety, and consideration for the creatures and their habitats. By following guidelines, practicing responsible behavior, and sharing our knowledge, we can enjoy these encounters while preserving the wonders of the natural world for generations to come.

First aid and emergency preparedness

Taking an RV trip is a fun way to discover new locations and make lifelong memories. But it's important to keep in mind that there are risks involved with traveling in an RV, just like there are with any outdoor activity. You and your fellow travelers' safety and well-being during your journey can be greatly enhanced by being ready for emergencies and possessing a thorough understanding of first aid. This section will cover the significance of emergency preparedness and first aid during an RV trip and offer insightful advice on how to be well-prepared and trained for unforeseen circumstances.

To begin with, accidents and medical emergencies can happen at any time, even when you are on the road. Whether it's a minor injury like a cut or a more serious incident such as heat exhaustion or a broken bone, having a well-stocked first aid kit on hand is essential. Your RV should have a comprehensive first aid kit that includes bandages, gauze, adhesive tape, antiseptic wipes, scissors, tweezers, pain relievers, and also any personal medications you or your travel companions may need. Regularly check and replenish the contents of your first aid kit to ensure that it is up-to-date and ready for use.

Additionally, it's crucial to have a basic understanding of first aid principles and techniques. Consider taking a first aid and CPR (or Cardiopulmonary Resuscitation) course before embarking on your RV adventure. These courses provide valuable knowledge on responding to various medical emergencies, including administering CPR, assisting choking victims, and addressing common injuries. Being well-versed in first aid can make a significant difference in providing immediate care while waiting for professional help to arrive.

Moreover, when traveling in an RV, it's essential to have a clear emergency plan in place. Ensure that all members of your travel group know the plan and how to contact emergency services for medical and non-medical emergencies. Keep a list of necessary contact numbers, including local hospitals, clinics, and emergency services, readily accessible. It's also a good idea to share your travel itinerary with a trusted friend or family member who can assist in case of emergency.

In addition to medical emergencies, RV travelers should be prepared for other unexpected situations, such as vehicle breakdowns or getting lost in unfamiliar terrain. Always carry essential supplies such as flashlights, batteries, a multi-tool kit, and a fully charged cell phone with a car charger. These items can be invaluable during unforeseen circumstances and can help you stay safe and self-reliant while awaiting assistance.

Furthermore, staying informed about the weather conditions and possible hazards in the areas you plan to visit is crucial for emergency preparedness. Check weather forecasts regularly and be mindful of any severe weather alerts or natural disasters that may affect your route. In case you encounter adverse weather conditions, have a plan for sheltering in your RV until it is safe to continue your journey. Familiarize yourself with evacuation routes as well as emergency shelters in the areas you will be traveling through.

Knowing the basics of RV maintenance and troubleshooting can also be a valuable asset during your adventure. Regularly inspect your RV for mechanical issues, and carry necessary tools and spare parts to address common problems. Familiarize yourself with the operation of your RV's systems, such as heating, cooling, and electrical systems, to avoid and address any issues that may arise during your travels.

In conclusion, first aid and emergency preparedness are paramount for a safe and enjoyable RV adventure. Accidents and unexpected situations can happen, but being equipped with the knowledge as well as resources to respond efficiently can make all the difference. Ensure your RV is stocked with a comprehensive first aid kit, takes first aid and CPR courses, and has a clear emergency plan in place. By prioritizing safety and preparedness, you can embark on your RV adventure with confidence, knowing that you are well-prepared to handle any unforeseen challenges that may arise along the way.

Communicating in remote areas

The chance to escape daily life's stress and savor the peace of nature is one of the main draws of an RV excursion. However, it's essential to balance the desire for solitude and the necessity of staying connected and informed, especially when traveling through remote or less populated areas. Effective communication in such regions is crucial for safety, navigation, and keeping in touch with loved ones. In this section, we will discuss the challenges of communicating in remote areas during an RV adventure and offer insights on ensuring reliable communication while preserving the essence of your journey.

Firstly, it's essential to acknowledge communication challenges in remote areas. Unlike urban environments where cell phone signals and Wi-Fi connectivity are readily available, remote regions often have limited or no access to these communication channels. This can pose difficulties in case of emergencies, navigation, or simply staying in contact with family and friends. Understanding the limitations of communication infrastructure in remote areas is the first step in addressing this challenge effectively.

To overcome these challenges, RV adventurers can employ various strategies and technologies to ensure reliable communication. One of the most accessible and versatile options is a satellite phone. Satellite phones operate independently of terrestrial cell towers, making them suitable for use in areas without cellular coverage. They provide voice and text communication, allowing you to stay in touch with emergency services, fellow travelers, and loved ones, even in the most remote locations.

Another valuable tool for communication in remote areas is a two-way radio or walkie-talkie. These devices are useful for short-range communication within your travel group or between vehicles. They can be convenient for coordinating activities, navigating tricky terrain, or communicating with weak or unavailable cell phone signals.

Furthermore, consider investing in a GPS device with satellite capabilities. These devices not only provide accurate navigation and mapping but also allow for two-way messaging in areas where traditional cell phone signals are absent. They can be a valuable asset for maintaining contact with emergency services or notifying others of your location in case of unforeseen circumstances.

Additionally, mobile hotspots or satellite internet solutions are available for those who rely on internet connectivity for work or staying in touch. While they may come at an extra cost, they provide access to the internet even in remote areas, allowing you to check emails, browse the web, and communicate via social media or messaging apps.

However, it's crucial to balance staying connected and fully immersing yourself in the RV adventure. The beauty of remote areas often lies in their pristine landscapes and the opportunity to disconnect from the digital world. While reliable communication is essential for safety, navigation, and emergencies, resist the urge to check your devices or engage in non-essential online activities constantly. Embrace the serenity and tranquility of remote locations by setting aside designated times for communication and digital use, allowing you to appreciate the natural wonders around you fully.

Lastly, research the communication options along your route when planning your RV adventure through remote areas. Be aware of any dead zones or areas with limited coverage, and plan accordingly. Give a reliable friend or family member access to your travel schedule so they can keep an eye on your progress and be informed of any emergencies or unplanned delays.

In conclusion, communicating in remote areas during an RV adventure presents challenges that require careful consideration and preparation. While technology offers an array of solutions to ensure reliable communication, it's essential to balance staying connected and fully experiencing the serenity of these pristine locations. By understanding the limitations of communication infrastructure, employing the right tools, and setting boundaries for digital usage, RV adventurers can navigate remote areas safely while preserving the essence of their journey.

CHAPTER XIII

RVing with Kids and Pets

Family-friendly RV trips

Embarking on an RV adventure with your family is a wonderful way to make lasting memories, strengthen bonds, and explore the beauty of the great outdoors together. Family-friendly RV trips offer the flexibility and comfort of a home on wheels while providing endless opportunities for adventure and learning. This section will explore the appeal of family-friendly RV trips and provide insights on planning a successful and enjoyable journey with your loved ones.

One of the primary advantages of family-friendly RV trips is their comfort and convenience. RVs are equipped with all the essentials for a comfortable journey, including sleeping quarters, a kitchen, and a bathroom. This means no more struggling with cramped car rides, limited restroom breaks, or the hassle of dining out. RVs provide a homey environment where you can relax, cook your own meals, and enjoy the freedom to come and go as you please.

Moreover, RV trips allow families to reconnect with nature and explore the great outdoors. From national parks to campgrounds nestled in scenic landscapes, RV travelers can access a wide range of natural wonders. Whether it's hiking through lush forests, swimming in crystal-clear lakes, or stargazing under the night sky, RV adventures allow families to appreciate the beauty and serenity of nature together.

RV trips also offer the flexibility to tailor your itinerary to suit your family's interests and preferences. You have the option of going to historical places, going on outdoor adventures, or just lounging around the campfire and spending time with each other. The freedom to change your plans on a whim and explore new destinations adds an element of spontaneity and excitement to your journey.

Additionally, RV trips promote learning and education in a fun and engaging way. Exploring different regions provides opportunities for children to learn about geography, history, and the natural world. Numerous locations that welcome RVs provide educational programs, guided tours, and practical experiences that can improve your family's understanding and admiration of the locations you visit.

Furthermore, RV trips encourage bonding and quality time with your family. You can engage in activities that foster closeness and shared experiences without distractions from screens or busy schedules. Whether it's cooking meals together, playing board games, or storytelling around the campfire, RV adventures provide the ideal backdrop for creating cherished family memories.

When planning a family-friendly RV trip, there are several key considerations to remember. First and foremost, involve your children in the planning process. Let them help choose destinations, activities, and even some of the meals you'll prepare together. Engaging your children in the planning phase can make them more excited and invested in the trip.

Next, prioritize safety by ensuring your RV is well-maintained and equipped with necessary safety features. Familiarize yourself and your family with emergency procedures, including fire safety and how to use safety equipment such as seatbelts and child car seats.

Pack strategically to make sure you have all the essentials for a comfortable journey. Don't forget to bring clothing appropriate for varying weather conditions, outdoor gear, and entertainment options for the family. A well-stocked RV can make a big difference in ensuring a smooth and enjoyable trip.

Finally, plan your route and itinerary to include a mix of activities and downtime. Be flexible with your schedule to allow unexpected discoveries or detours along the way. Remember that the journey is as important as the destination, so savor the moments spent together on the road.

In conclusion, family-friendly RV trips offer a unique blend of comfort, adventure, and quality time that can create unforgettable experiences for your loved ones. These journeys provide opportunities for learning, bonding, and exploring the beauty of the natural world. By involving your family in planning and prioritizing safety and preparation, you can embark on a successful and enjoyable RV adventure that strengthens family ties and creates lasting memories.

Tips for traveling with children

Embarking on an RV adventure with your children can be an exciting as well as memorable experience, offering family bonding and exploration opportunities. However, traveling with kids in an RV comes with unique challenges and considerations. To ensure a successful and enjoyable journey, it's essential to plan ahead and be prepared. This section will provide valuable tips for traveling with children on RV trips, helping you create lasting memories while keeping everyone comfortable and safe.

Firstly, involve your children in the trip planning process. Allow them to have a say in choosing destinations, activities, and even the route you'll take. This sense of involvement and ownership can excite and engage them throughout the journey. Discuss the itinerary together and explain what they can expect at each stop, fostering a sense of anticipation and adventure.

Pack strategically to make sure you have all the essentials for your children's comfort and entertainment. Bring clothing suitable for varying weather conditions, including layers and rain gear. Don't forget outdoor gear such as bicycles, scooters, or hiking equipment to keep them active and engaged during stops. Consider their favorite toys, books, and games to provide entertainment during downtime.

Safety should be a top priority when traveling with children in an RV. Ensure that your RV is equipped with the necessary safety features, including seatbelts, child car seats, and childproofing measures. Familiarize your children with emergency procedures, such as what to do in case of a fire or a medical emergency. Review safety rules for both inside and outside the RV to prevent accidents during the trip.

Plan your travel days strategically to accommodate your children's needs. RV travel allows for flexibility, so plan shorter driving distances each day and include frequent breaks for stretching, bathroom breaks, and snacks. Take advantage of scenic rest stops and parks for outdoor playtime to let them burn off energy.

Create a comfortable sleeping arrangement for your children in the RV. RVs come in various sizes and configurations, so choose one that best suits your family's needs. Bunk beds, convertible dinettes, or separate sleeping areas can provide your children a sense of personal space and comfort. Be sure to pack their favorite bedding and stuffed animals to make them feel at home.

Keep a well-stocked supply of snacks and drinks readily available. Hungry and thirsty kids can become cranky quickly, so having a variety of healthy snacks and beverages on hand can help avoid meltdowns. Consider a designated snack box or bag that your children can access easily during the journey.

Entertainment is key to keeping children engaged during long stretches of driving. Pack a selection of their favorite movies, audiobooks, music, and electronic devices with headphones. Additionally, encourage activities involving the whole family, such as playing travel games, singing songs, or spotting wildlife and interesting landmarks.

Plan your RV stops with your children's interests in mind. Research family-friendly attractions, parks, and activities at each destination. Look for educational opportunities that can enrich their understanding of the places you visit, such as museums, historical sites, and nature centers. Engaging them in the exploration and learning process can make the trip even more rewarding for everyone.

Finally, maintain open communication with your children throughout the journey. Invite them to express their emotions, ideas, and experiences. Be patient and flexible in addressing their needs and concerns, and remember that unexpected challenges may arise. Emphasize the importance of teamwork and cooperation within the family to create a harmonious and enjoyable RV adventure.

In conclusion, traveling with children on RV trips can be a fulfilling and enriching experience that creates lasting family memories. You can guarantee a successful and enjoyable journey by involving your children in the planning process, prioritizing safety, packing strategically, and providing ample entertainment and educational opportunities. With the right preparation and a positive attitude, your RV adventure with your children can become a cherished and unforgettable experience for the entire family.

Pet-friendly National Parks and RVing

For many pet owners, their furry companions are an integral part of the family. When it comes to planning an RV adventure, the desire to bring your pet along for the journey is entirely understandable. Fortunately, numerous pet-friendly national parks and campgrounds across the United States welcome you and your four- legged friend. In this section, we will explore the appeal of pet-friendly national parks and offer insights on how to enjoy an RV trip with your pet while respecting the park's regulations and preserving the natural environment.

The allure of pet-friendly national parks lies in the opportunity to explore the stunning beauty and rich biodiversity of these protected areas alongside your beloved pet. From the majestic mountains to lush forests and pristine lakes, national parks offer a wide range of natural wonders that can be shared and appreciated together. Hiking scenic trails, picnicking by a river, or simply enjoying the tranquility of the great outdoors becomes even more enjoyable when your pet is by your side.

When planning an RV trip with your pet, it's essential to research and choose national parks and campgrounds that are pet-friendly. Not all parks have the same rules and regulations regarding pets, so make sure to check the particular guidelines of the park you plan to visit. Most pet-friendly national parks require pets to be kept on a leash at all times and prohibit them from entering certain areas, such as visitor centers, backcountry trails, and wildlife habitats. Familiarizing yourself with these rules ensures a smooth and enjoyable experience for both you and your pet.

Additionally, consider the comfort and safety of your pet while traveling in your RV. Ensure that your RV is equipped with appropriate accommodations for your pet, such as a secure area for them to rest and travel comfortably. Pack all the essential supplies, including food, water, bedding, and any medications your pet may require. Regularly check that your pet is well-hydrated, especially during warm weather, and provide ample opportunities for exercise and bathroom breaks during your stops.

When exploring national parks with your pet, practice responsible pet ownership. Clean up after your pet by bringing waste disposal bags and disposing of waste in designated receptacles. Respect wildlife as well as their habitats by maintaining a safe distance and not allowing your pet to chase or disturb wildlife. Ensure that your pet's behavior is considerate of other visitors, and be prepared to control and calm your pet if they become agitated or anxious in crowded or unfamiliar environments.

Furthermore, take advantage of the numerous pet-friendly activities available in national parks. Many parks offer pet-friendly trails for hiking and walking, allowing you to explore the area's natural beauty while your pet enjoys the fresh air and exercise. Be mindful of the park's regulations regarding pets on trails, and always keep your pet on a leash where required.

Before your RV adventure, visit your veterinarian to make sure your pet is in good health and up-to-date on vaccinations. Discuss any specific concerns or considerations about your pet's well-being during the trip, and ask for recommendations on managing travel-related stress or motion sickness. Carry your pet's medical records, identification, and contact information for your veterinarian in case of emergencies.

In conclusion, pet-friendly national parks and RVing offer a unique and fulfilling way to explore the natural beauty of the United States with your furry companion. By researching and adhering to park regulations, ensuring the comfort as well as safety of your pet during the journey, and practicing responsible pet ownership, you can enjoy a memorable and harmonious RV adventure with your beloved pet. The joy of sharing the wonders of the great outdoors with your pet creates lasting memories and strengthens the bond between you and your four- legged family member.

CHAPTER XIV

Sustainable RV Travel

Reducing your carbon footprint while RVing

RVing offers a unique and adventurous way to explore the world around us, but it's essential to be mindful of the environmental impact of this travel mode. While RVs provide the freedom to roam and enjoy the beauty of nature, they also consume resources and produce emissions. However, there are steps you can take to reduce your carbon footprint while RVing, making your journeys more sustainable and eco-friendly.

Firstly, consider your choice of RV. Smaller and more fuel-efficient models can help reduce fuel consumption and emissions. Opt for an RV with modern, energy-efficient appliances and systems, such as LED lighting, solar panels, and efficient heating and cooling systems. These features reduce your energy consumption and save you money in the long run.

When it comes to driving your RV, adopting eco-friendly driving habits can make a significant difference. Drive at a moderate speed and keep a steady pace to maximize fuel efficiency. Avoid idling your engine unnecessarily, as it wastes fuel and emits pollutants. Properly inflate your tires to the recommended levels to mitigate rolling resistance and enhance fuel economy.

Planning your RV routes strategically can also help reduce your carbon footprint. Opt for shorter and more direct routes, avoiding congested highways and heavy traffic whenever possible. Research campgrounds and RV parks that promote eco-friendly practices, such as recycling and energy conservation, and support their efforts during your stays.

Minimize your energy consumption while parked by being mindful of your RV's power usage. Turn off lights, appliances, and electronics when not in use. Consider using energy-efficient LED or solar-powered lights to reduce electricity consumption. Use natural ventilation and insulation to maintain a comfortable temperature inside your RV, reducing the need for heating or cooling.

Reduce waste generation by practicing responsible waste management while RVing. Use reusable containers and utensils, and avoid single-use plastics whenever possible. Sort recyclables from trash and place them in designated containers at recycling centers or campgrounds. Composting food scraps is another eco-friendly option to reduce waste.

Water conservation is crucial when RVing to minimize your impact on the environment. Install low-flow faucets and showerheads in your RV to reduce water consumption. Be mindful of water usage while showering, washing dishes, and doing laundry. Collect rainwater for outdoor use, like watering plants or cleaning your RV, if allowed in the area you visit.

Support sustainable and eco-friendly campgrounds and RV parks that prioritize environmental stewardship. These establishments often implement water and energy conservation, recycling programs, and habitat preservation practices. By staying at such locations, you can contribute to their efforts and reduce your environmental impact.

Explore your surroundings responsibly by following Leave No Trace principles. Stay on designated trails, respect wildlife and their habitats, and avoid disturbing natural ecosystems. In order to protect the beauty of the natural environment for future generations of RV enthusiasts, dispose of garbage properly and pack out all trash.

To produce clean energy, think about adding green technology to your RV, like solar or wind turbines. These renewable energy sources can power your RV's appliances and reduce your reliance on fossil fuels.

Lastly, educate yourself and your fellow travelers about the importance of eco-friendly RVing practices. Share information on reducing carbon footprints, conserving resources, and protecting the environment with other RV enthusiasts you meet on the road. Encourage responsible and sustainable RVing within your community and social networks.

In conclusion, reducing your carbon footprint while RVing benefits the environment and allows you to enjoy your adventures with a greater sense of eco-consciousness. By making mindful choices regarding your RV, driving habits, energy consumption, waste management, and campground selection, you can mitigate the impact of your travels and contribute to a more sustainable and enjoyable RVing experience.

Eco-friendly camping practices

Camping in an RV offers the opportunity to immerse yourself in the beauty of nature while also enjoying the comforts of home on wheels. However, with this convenience comes the responsibility to minimize your environmental impact and practice eco-friendly camping. By adopting sustainable practices, RV enthusiasts can contribute to preserving natural landscapes and protecting the environment for future generations. In this section, we will explore eco-friendly camping practices specific to RVing and how you can positively impact the environment while enjoying the great outdoors.

One of the basic principles of eco-friendly camping in an RV is reducing your energy consumption. RVs are equipped with various appliances and systems, from refrigerators to heating and cooling, that can consume significant energy. To minimize your carbon footprint, opt for energy-efficient appliances and LED lighting. Installing solar panels on your RV can assist you become less dependent on conventional power sources and fossil fuels by capturing clean, renewable energy from the sun.

Another essential component of eco-friendly RV camping is water conservation. Utilizing water wisely is crucial because most RVs have a limited water supply. Minimize water usage by installing low-flow showerheads and faucets, and stop leaks as soon as possible to avoid wasting water. To reduce your impact on the environment, use less water when taking showers, cleaning dishes, and doing laundry. You can also use eco-friendly and biodegradable cleaning products.

An essential part of eco-friendly RV camping is waste management. Use reusable utensils and containers to reduce the amount of waste you produce, and steer clear of single-use plastics whenever you can. At recycling centers or campgrounds, separate recyclables from trash and place them in appropriate containers. One environmentally friendly way to drastically cut down on the quantity of organic waste you produce while camping is by composting food scraps.

Another essential practice for eco-friendly RV camping is ethical sewage disposal. RVs have wastewater tanks that require proper handling and disposal. Always use designated dumping stations or sewer connections at campgrounds to dispose of blackwater and graywater. Never dump wastewater onto the ground or into natural water bodies, as it can contaminate the environment and harm aquatic ecosystems.

When selecting campgrounds and RV parks, choose eco-friendly establishments prioritizing environmental stewardship. Many campgrounds implement sustainable practices such as water and energy conservation, recycling programs, and habitat preservation. Staying at such locations reduces your environmental impact and directly supports their conservation efforts.

Transportation is a significant consideration for eco-friendly camping in an RV. While driving to your destination, adopt eco-friendly driving habits to minimize fuel consumption and emissions. Drive at moderate speeds, maintain a steady pace, and avoid unnecessary idling. Properly inflate your tires to reduce rolling resistance and improve fuel economy.

Additionally, plan your routes strategically to minimize driving distances and avoid congested highways whenever possible. Opt for shorter and more direct routes to reduce fuel consumption and emissions. Consider using alternative transportation methods, like bicycles or public transit, to explore your destination once you've parked your RV.

Responsible outdoor exploration is essential for eco-friendly RV camping. Follow Leave No Trace principles to mitigate your effect on the environment. Stay on designated trails, avoid disturbing wildlife, and pack out all trash and waste. Respect natural ecosystems and wildlife habitats to ensure they remain pristine and undisturbed.

Finally, engage with local communities and support businesses prioritizing sustainable and eco-friendly practices. Purchase goods and services from local providers prioritizing environmentally responsible and ethical practices. By contributing to the economic well-being of these communities, you indirectly support their conservation efforts and commitment to sustainable living.

In conclusion, eco-friendly camping practices in an RV involve conscious choices that minimize your environmental impact while enjoying the beauty of the outdoors. By reducing energy consumption, conserving water, practicing responsible waste management, choosing eco-friendly campgrounds, adopting eco-friendly driving habits, following Leave No Trace principles, and supporting local communities, you can make a meaningful difference in preserving natural landscapes and protecting the environment. Eco-friendly camping is a shared responsibility, and each of us has a role to play in ensuring the sustainability of our outdoor adventures.

Supporting conservation efforts

Embarking on an RV adventure offers a unique opportunity to connect with nature and explore the great outdoors. However, it's essential to recognize that our natural resources and ecosystems need protection and conservation. When we RV responsibly, we can support conservation efforts and have a positive impact. In this section, we will explore how RV enthusiasts can contribute to the preservation of our environment and biodiversity.

One of the most straightforward ways to support conservation efforts while RVing is by minimizing your environmental footprint. Reduce your energy consumption by using LED lighting, energy-efficient appliances, and renewable energy sources including solar panels. Be mindful of water usage and waste generation by conserving water and practicing responsible waste management, including recycling and composting. Additionally, adopt eco-friendly driving habits to reduce fuel consumption and emissions while on the road.

Another way to support conservation is by choosing eco-friendly campgrounds and RV parks. Many of these establishments prioritize environmental stewardship by implementing sustainable practices including water and energy conservation, recycling programs, and habitat preservation. Staying at such locations minimizes your impact and directly supports their conservation efforts.

Participating in organized clean-up events and volunteer programs is another excellent way to contribute to conservation while RVing. Many national parks, forests, and wildlife reserves organize clean-up days and volunteer opportunities for visitors. These activities may involve litter removal, trail maintenance, habitat restoration, and wildlife monitoring. By volunteering your time and effort, you actively contribute to preserving these natural spaces.

Supporting conservation organizations and initiatives financially is also a meaningful way to make a difference. Consider donating to reputable organizations dedicated to environmental protection, wildlife conservation, and habitat restoration. Many of these organizations work tirelessly to safeguard our natural heritage, and your contributions can help fund vital conservation projects.

Educating yourself and your fellow travelers about local ecosystems, wildlife, and conservation issues is essential for making a positive impact. Attend ranger-led programs, visitor center exhibits, and guided tours in national parks and wildlife reserves to learn more regarding the environment and conservation efforts in the region you are exploring. Share your knowledge with fellow RV enthusiasts and encourage responsible and environmentally conscious practices within your community.

When exploring natural areas, follow Leave No Trace principles to minimize your environmental impact. Stay on designated trails, avoid disturbing wildlife, and pack out all trash and waste. Respecting natural ecosystems and following ethical wildlife viewing guidelines ensures the environment remains pristine and undisturbed.

Additionally, support local communities that rely on sustainable and eco-friendly practices. Purchase goods and services from local businesses prioritizing environmentally responsible and ethical practices. By contributing to the economic well-being of these communities, you indirectly support their conservation efforts and commitment to sustainable living.

Conservation efforts extend beyond protecting natural spaces and include safeguarding cultural and historical heritage. When visiting areas of cultural significance, respect historical sites and artifacts, and follow preservation guidelines. By appreciating and preserving both natural and cultural heritage, you help ensure a rich and diverse tapestry of history and tradition for future generations.

Finally, advocate for policies and practices that promote conservation at local, state, and national levels. Engage with government agencies, legislators, and advocacy groups to voice your support for environmental protection, wildlife conservation, and sustainable practices. Encourage responsible land use and policies that prioritize the preservation of natural areas and biodiversity.

In conclusion, RV enthusiasts have the power to support conservation efforts and take part to the protection of our environment and natural resources. By minimizing your environmental footprint, choosing eco-friendly campgrounds, volunteering, donating, educating yourself and others, practicing Leave No Trace principles, supporting local communities, and advocating for conservation policies, you can make a meaningful difference while enjoying the beauty of the outdoors during your RV adventures. Conservation is a shared responsibility, and each of us has a role to play in preserving the natural world for future generations.

CHAPTER XV

Wrapping Up Your Adventure

Closing thoughts on RVing in National Parks

RVing in national parks is a truly remarkable way to connect with the beauty of our natural world, immerse yourself in diverse ecosystems, and create lasting memories with loved ones. Throughout this section, we have explored the numerous benefits and considerations of RVing in national parks, from the sense of freedom and flexibility it offers to the need for responsible and eco-friendly practices. As we conclude our discussion, it's important to reflect on the unique opportunities and responsibilities of exploring these pristine landscapes.

First and foremost, RVing in national parks allows you to experience the splendor of the great outdoors like no other form of travel. From towering peaks of the Rocky Mountains to the lush forests of the Smokies and the striking canyons of the Southwest, national parks showcase the diversity and majesty of our natural world. The freedom to camp amidst this breathtaking scenery, wake up to the songs of birds, and witness wildlife in its natural habitat is a privilege that RV enthusiasts cherish.

But this privilege also carries a duty to safeguard and maintain these delicate ecosystems. National parks are sanctuaries for biodiversity, providing refuge for countless plant and animal species. RVers must adhere to strict regulations and ethical principles to ensure minimal disruption to these environments. By following Leave No Trace principles, practicing responsible waste management, and respecting park rules, we can help safeguard these precious landscapes for future generations.

Moreover, RVing in national parks offers personal growth and education opportunities. Exploring these protected areas' rich geological features, cultural history, and ecological diversity deepens our understanding of the world around us. It fosters an appreciation for these parks' natural and cultural heritage, instilling a sense of stewardship and commitment to their conservation.

The sense of community among RV enthusiasts in national parks is also worth noting. Fellow travelers often share a common love for nature and a passion for outdoor adventures. Exchanging stories, tips, and experiences with fellow RVers can enrich your journey and create connections that endure long after your RV adventure has concluded.

In conclusion, RVing in national parks is a unique and enriching experience that allows you to immerse yourself in the beauty of our natural world while enjoying the comforts of home on wheels. It offers the flexibility to travel to various locations, establish a connection with the natural world, and make priceless memories with loved ones. But it's imperative that you approach this adventure with a strong sense of environmental responsibility. We can make sure that future generations can enjoy the wonder and majesty of our national parks by camping sustainably, adhering to park rules, and supporting conservation efforts. RVing in national parks is not just a journey but a commitment to preserving the natural treasures that define our nation and an enduring appreciation for the remarkable world we inhabit.

Tips for post-trip maintenance and cleaning

As you wrap up your RV adventure and return from your travels, it's essential to pay attention to post-trip maintenance and cleaning to ensure your RV's longevity and proper functioning. Proper care not only extends the life of your vehicle but also ensures a comfortable and pleasant experience on your next journey. This section will discuss valuable tips for post-trip maintenance and cleaning of your RV to keep it in optimal condition.

Start with a thorough exterior cleaning. Road dust, dirt, and grime can accumulate on the exterior of your RV during your travels. Use a mild detergent or RV-specific cleaning solution to wash the exterior, paying particular attention to areas such as the roof, awnings, and windows. Scrubbing is best done with a soft brush or sponge to prevent scratching the paint or finish. After giving the outside a thorough rinse to get rid of any soap residue, think about using a wax or sealant to preserve the appearance and protect it.

Next, look for any indications of wear or damage on the RV's roof. It's imperative to maintain the condition of your RV's roof because it serves as a vital shield against the weather. Examine the roofing material for any cracks, leaks, or loose seams, and take quick action to fix any problems you find. To avoid clogs in the gutters and drains, remove any dirt, leaves, or branches from the roof.

Check the RV's tires for proper inflation and wear. Overinflated or underinflated tires can affect your RV's handling and fuel efficiency. Ensure that the tires are inflated to the manufacturer's recommended pressure and inspect them for signs of damage or excessive wear. Consider rotating the tires and having them balanced and aligned if necessary. Proper tire maintenance is necessary for safety and performance during your next adventure.

Inspect the RV's undercarriage and chassis for any signs of wear, damage, or corrosion. This includes checking the suspension, brakes, axles, and other components that ensure the RV's stability and safety on the road. If you observe any issues, consult with a professional RV mechanic for a thorough inspection and necessary repairs.

Don't forget to attend to the RV's interior. Vacuum and clean all surfaces, including floors, carpets, upholstery, and countertops. Wipe down all cabinets, appliances, and fixtures with a suitable cleaning solution, taking care to remove any food crumbs or residues. Check and clean or replace air filters in heating and cooling systems to ensure proper ventilation and air quality inside the RV.

Inspect the RV's plumbing and electrical systems for any leaks or malfunctions. Check for loose connections, damaged hoses, or corroded pipes in the plumbing system. Test all electrical outlets, switches, and appliances to ensure they are functioning correctly. Replace any faulty components or seek professional assistance if needed.

If your RV has a generator, perform routine maintenance as the manufacturer recommends. This may include replacing filters, changing the oil, and checking for any generator operation issues. A well-maintained generator ensures a reliable source of power during your travels.

Address any pest control concerns. RVs can sometimes be susceptible to pests like ants, rodents, or insects. Preventive measures include sealing entry points, storing food properly, and using pest repellents to deter unwanted visitors. Inspect the interior for signs of pests, and if necessary, consult with a professional exterminator to address infestations.

Finally, consider the RV's storage needs. Proper storage during the off-season or between trips is essential for preserving its condition. Store your RV in a dry, sheltered location to protect it from the elements. Cover it with an RV cover to shield it from UV rays, dirt, and debris. If your RV has a battery, disconnect it to prevent draining during storage, and consider using stabilizers to prevent flat spots on the tires.

In conclusion, post-trip maintenance and RV cleaning are crucial steps to ensure your vehicle's continued enjoyment and reliability. A well-maintained RV enhances your comfort on the road and minimizes the risk of costly repairs and breakdowns. By following these tips and dealing with any issues promptly, you can keep your RV in optimal condition and be ready for your next adventure with peace of mind.

Planning your next RV adventure

Arranging an RV trip can be a thrilling undertaking that provides endless opportunities for discovery and excitement. Whether you're an experienced RV traveler or a beginner looking to take your first trip, careful planning is necessary to guarantee a hassle-free and joyful experience. In this section we will explore the key steps and considerations for planning your next RV adventure, from choosing destinations to preparing your vehicle and establishing an itinerary that suits your interests.

The initial step in planning your RV adventure is selecting your destination(s). Consider your interests and preferences. Do you yearn for the beauty of national parks, the serenity of coastal campgrounds, or the excitement of bustling cities? Research potential destinations, considering the time of year, weather conditions, and any special events or attractions you want to experience. Create a list of must-see places and prioritize them based on your interests and available time.

Once you've chosen your destinations, determine your route. RV travel provides the flexibility to choose your own path, so plan a route that takes you through scenic landscapes and intriguing stops along the way. Use maps,

GPS navigation systems, or RV trip planning apps to plot your course, and take into account alternate routes in case of road closures or unexpected detours. Factor in driving times and distances to ensure a comfortable pace that allows for rest stops and exploration.

Now it's time to prepare your RV for the journey. Perform a thorough inspection of your vehicle, inspecting for any indications of damage, wear, or malfunction. Ensure that all essential systems, including the engine, brakes, tires, and plumbing, are in good working order. Make any necessary repairs or maintenance before hitting the road to minimize the risk of breakdowns during your trip. Don't forget to check safety equipment such as fire extinguishers, smoke detectors, as well as carbon monoxide detectors.

Stock your RV with all the essentials you'll need for the journey. Create a checklist that includes bedding, towels, toiletries, kitchen supplies, and any personal items you can't do without. Consider the particular needs of your trip, such as outdoor gear, recreational equipment, or pet supplies if you're traveling with pets. Remember that RVs have limited storage space, so pack efficiently and prioritize items based on necessity.

Safety is paramount during an RV adventure, so be sure to review and refresh your knowledge of RV safety practices. Ensure that all passengers are familiar with emergency procedures, including fire safety and how to use safety equipment like seatbelts and child car seats. If you're new to RVing, consider taking a driving safety course to become more comfortable handling and maneuvering your vehicle.

When planning your itinerary, strike a balance between scheduled activities and flexibility. Leave room for spontaneity and unexpected discoveries along the way. Consider the interests of all travelers in your group and plan activities that cater to each person's preferences.

Whether it's hiking, fishing, visiting museums, or simply relaxing by the campfire, tailor your itinerary to create a well-rounded as well as enjoyable experience for everyone.

One of the joys of RV travel is the opportunity to immerse yourself in the natural world. Research campgrounds, RV parks, and boondocking opportunities in your chosen destinations. Some travelers prefer the amenities of RV parks, while others enjoy the solitude and natural settings of boondocking. Reserve campsites in advance, particularly during peak seasons, to ensure you have a place to stay at your preferred locations.

Budgeting for your RV adventure is a critical aspect of planning. Calculate the fuel costs, campground fees, food, activities, and any additional expenses associated with your trip. Consider putting aside a contingency fund for emergencies or unforeseen repairs, and be ready for unexpected expenses. Making a budget guarantees that you have the money to enjoy your trip stress-free and helps you keep track of your spending.

Create a list of the necessary paperwork and documents for your trip at the end. This covers your driver's license, insurance and registration for your car, health insurance cards, and any permits or passes required for visiting national parks or engaging in recreational activities. Throughout your trip, keep these documents accessible and well-organized.

In conclusion, planning your next RV adventure is a rewarding process that allows you to create lasting memories and explore the beauty of our world. By carefully choosing your destinations, preparing your RV, creating a well-thought-out itinerary, and considering safety and budgeting, you can embark on a journey filled with excitement and adventure. Whether you're traveling solo, with family, or with friends, the planning process is an essential part of the adventure that sets the stage for a memorable and fulfilling RV journey.

CONCLUSION

In conclusion, "Wheels and Wilderness: The Ultimate RV Guide to National Park Adventures" is a comprehensive and invaluable resource for anyone seeking to embark on the exciting journey of RV travel through America's stunning national parks. Throughout this book, we've explored every facet of the RV adventure, from selecting the perfect RV for your needs to planning an unforgettable itinerary, making campground reservations, packing essentials, and ensuring safety on the road.

This guide has given you essential knowledge on RV types, budgeting, and financing options, detailed insights into researching and exploring national parks, and practical tips on creating itineraries, packing lists, and acquiring must-have camping gear. We've also covered crucial aspects of safety equipment, pre-trip inspections, and troubleshooting common RV issues to ensure that your journey is as safe as it is enjoyable.

With "Wheels and Wilderness" as your trusted companion, you have the tools and guidance to begin on an epic RV adventure, immersing yourself in America's national parks' natural beauty and wonders. Whether you're a seasoned RVer or a newcomer to this exhilarating lifestyle, this book has empowered you with the knowledge and confidence to explore the wilderness, discover new horizons, and create cherished memories that will last a lifetime.

So, fuel up your RV, plan your route, and set out on the open road with "Wheels and Wilderness" as your guide, as the boundless beauty of national parks and the thrill of RV travel await you, promising a journey filled with wonder, adventure, and the freedom to roam.

Thank you for buying and reading/ listening to our book. If you found this book useful/ helpful please take a few minutes and leave a review on the platform where you purchased our book. Your feedback matters greatly to us.